By Kevin Toolis

Rebel Hearts: Journeys Within the IRA's Soul

MY
FATHER'S
WAKE

MY FATHER'S WAKE

HOW THE IRISH TEACH US TO LIVE, LOVE AND DIE

KEVIN TOOLIS

Da Capo Press

Da Capo Press
Hachette Book Group
1290 Avenue of the Americas, New York, NY 10104
www.dacapopress.com
@DaCapoPress; @DaCapoPR

Printed in the United States of America

Originally published in Great Britain in 2017 by Weidenfeld & Nicolson, an imprint of The Orion Publishing Group, Ltd., a Hachette UK Company

First U.S. Edition: September 2017
Published by Da Capo Press, an imprint of Perseus Books, LLC, a subsidiary of Hachette Book Group, Inc. The Da Capo name and logo is a trademark of the Hachette Book Group.

The publisher is not responsible for websites (or their content) that are not owned by the publisher.

Typeset by Input Data Services, Ltd., Somerset, Great Britain

Library of Congress Cataloging-in-Publication Data has been applied for.
ISBNs: 978-0-306-92146-9 (hardcover); 978-0-306-92145-2 (ebook)
LCCN: 2017948124

LSC-C

10   9   8   7   6   5   4   3   2   1

For Sonny, and other keepers of an ancient faith,
and Dea, who never stopped believing.

CONTENTS

'The generations of men are like generations of leaves. The wind scatters one year's leaves down on to the earth, but when spring comes the luxuriant forest produces other leaves; so it is with the generations of men, one grows as the other comes to end.'

Iliad, 6–145

MORTALITIES

In the narrow room the old man lay close to death.

Two days before he had ceased to speak, lapsed into unconsciousness, and the final vigil had begun. The ravages of cancer had eaten into the muscle, leaving a starved skeletal husk. In the bed the body lay awkwardly propped; the skull and limbs crucified at jarring angles. The open eyes were cloudy, their tissues dried; the seized mouth a scabby parched red hole. The heart beat on and the lungs drew breath but it was impossible to tell if he remained aware. Above the man's head, to the right on the whitewashed wall, a cheap print of a ruddy-faced Jesus Christ, his heart exposed and arms outstretched, offered eternal salvation to his followers.

Just after dawn on the longest day, the breathing grew hectic. The skeletal ribcage heaved with irregular breath, the wheezing lungs gasping for oxygen, failing into silence and then, against expectation, rising again. The death rattle had commenced. The *bean chaointe* pronounced; the moment of death was close. A nine-year-old boy was hurriedly despatched to gather in the last of the man's sons. Boy and son returned to find ten watchers crammed shoulder tight within the spartan room, all staring at the tangle of limbs. A rasping breathing filled the air.

Huh, huh, huh.

In the silence of the watchers . . . *huh, huh, huh* . . . that panicked drowning sound . . . *huh, huh, huh, huh, huh, huh, HUH, HUH, HUH* . . . rose to a crescendo then plummeted, free-falling, into an agonising void.

And then began again.

Huh, huh, huh . . .

This death was not veiled but a rite within an Irish clan.

I stared around the room at these watchers: at my nine-year-old nephew Séan who had come for me; at my heavily pregnant cousin Bernadette; at the seer, my matronly Aunt Tilda who now led us in the wake, the woman of wounds, our midwife of death; at Nora, the elderly neighbour who sold eggs; and at other witnesses to whom I had never spoken. I wondered what they sought to gain from the moment of death of this man. Of Sonny. My father.

The seer broke out in prayer and began to recite the Five Sorrowful Mysteries of the Rosary.

Hail Mary, full of grace, the Lord is with thee, blessed art thou amongst women, and blessed is the fruit of thy womb, Jesus.

As one, the watchers returned her chant. The tight single-bedded room, no bigger than a prison cell, filled up; the song of voices overwhelming the stuttering rhythm of Sonny's lungs.

Holy Mary, Mother of God, pray for us sinners now and at the hour of our death.

The sound boomed off the ceiling, off the white-washed walls, the concrete floor, the glass cover of Jesus Our Saviour, reverberating, louder and louder, filling every orifice.

Hail Mary, full of grace, the Lord is with thee, blessed art thou, amongst women and blessed is the fruit of thy womb Jesus. Holy Mary, Mother of God, pray for us sinners now and at the hour of our death.

Verse, after verse, prayer after prayer. Keening.

For years as a child, in one gloomy Catholic church after another, I recited that prayer, running the words together like a hollowed verbal conjuring trick until I could say *HolyMaryMotherofGodprayforus . . . sinners now . . . andatthehour . . . ofourdeath* in four seconds flat.

Words breathed but emptied of meaning.

Now, I was home on the island off the coast of Ireland's poorest county, Mayo, in the furthest western reaches of Europe, for the hour of this death.

Home on an island of elemental fury, a rock citadel in the great ocean, where huge Atlantic storms break onshore, scouring the landscape and destroying everything not anchored down. The wind howling, wailing, car-door-wrenching. At night as you lie in bed

awake, the storm surging in assault, striking at the rat-
tling roof, the shaking windows, to suck you out, every
living soul within, up into the maelstrom. The great
ocean, a hundred yards away, was alive and malevo-
lent, the surf a cascading white fury. The waves lashing
every headland, surging, turning, daring you just close
enough to capture you for the depths. My godfather,
a shepherd, and two of his companions were swept to
their deaths rescuing sheep on what had started as a
clear winter's day.

And with the wind comes the rain. Bucketing,
drenching rain, for months on end. Swallowing the
ocean, the earth, the hills, the horizon, in a bleary,
grey stinging assault. Pouring, pouring, from the
sky in deluge. Black mile-high sheets of falling water
sweeping in from the western horizon, bursting on the
sodden earth before roaring back down heather hillsides into the ocean. The sky too another vast ocean;
often grey or darkening black with rain-laden clouds,
but sometimes pink, scarlet red or blue. Or shimmering
with light as sun-lanced pillars of gold burst through
an overcast sky onto grey waters. Or the air filling up
with mist showers and the whole world, sea, sky, earth,
glimmering back in a mirror of silver light.

And then there are days when the sun blazes as a
God chariot rising from behind Minaun mountain over
the ocean in a great arc before descending in a blood
red orb into the ocean behind Croaghaun mountain.

Yellow lilacs rocket skywards from the bog, and meadows sway with golden buttercups and white daisies. The sea turns green glass, the wind stills, and dolphins leap in the surf so close to shore you could easily swim out to them. Like a smoky perfume, the smell of peat turf lazily drifts over the village and the blue-eyed sheepdogs of Dookinella deliciously spread themselves on the tar and gravel road to cool their molten bodies.

As Sonny lay dying we had another kind of weather: humid, hazy days, the entire village consumed in sea mist. We were unable to see further than the garden gate: all land, sea and sky shrouded in a still blanket that made night and day one. We were becalmed. Waiting for his heart to stop, the wake, his funeral, the church, the grave. Waiting for the death of this very ordinary man. Waiting, I thought, to start again. Resume Life. As it turned out, nothing else I have ever done or will do was more important than those precious days.

I had come home to the island, and our village, Dookinella, *Dumha Cionn Aille* in Irish, the sandy bank at the head of the cliff, nestled on the foreshore of the great Atlantic Ocean. An island furthest to the west, closer to the sunset. Home to an arcadia of small farms and wild mountains, where the roar of ocean surf never ceases and flocks of sheep wander freely on the roads; migrating nightly along the ocean's edge to pasture on the hills, before returning in a dawn pilgrimage to the sweet grasses of the lake shore. Passing tractor drivers on the road, their narrow cabs crammed either with small children or dogs, sometimes both, wave a friendly salute to oncoming cars for no real reason other than to say hello.

Returning to a village where the last roads of Europe ran out into the ocean and the same dogs lie in wait in the long grass by the side of road guarding passage. Barking and chasing after strange cars as if driving out a foreign enemy. Home to the stone ruins of the past, the old clachans of drystone houses broken open to the elements, their descendants scattered across the face of the Earth. I was back in a patchwork of tiny green fields, divided and further subdivided for the last 200 years. Home to a house built by Sonny and my grandfather Patrick in the 1930s. I was standing in the same white-washed room where my mother, Mary Gallagher, had given birth to my brother, standing too amongst the watchers, and where Sonny now lay dying. Home to a village where the bloodlines crossed and mixed generation after generation, and where our own small sept, clan, was part of the very naming of the land, Dookinelly Thulis, in the first nineteenth-century maps.

And the line of my fathers and mothers, and their forefathers and foremothers, ran back three centuries.

I was related in blood to all of these watchers, though many of them I barely knew and could never recall their names. Some I had met as a teenager at the local dances, at Mass, walking back the shore, at weddings and in the local bars. I stumbled before their profuse 'Welcome home's, their easy grace of kinship, their uncontrived acceptance of my life beyond the island – failure or success. And their uncanny ability to name me and chart the genealogical web – cousin, second cousin, second cousin to your grandfather – that we shared.

Holy Mary . . .

Yet I was a stranger here, a traitor in my Irish skin. As a child and teenager I had spent every summer 'home' on the island, roaming the beaches, working on the bog or making hay, drinking in the bars or riding pillion on Padraig Mac's Honda to distant dance halls – the Wavecrest, the Valley or the shed-like Bunacurry Ballroom – in search of teenage romance. I even had a few island girlfriends. But amidst these watchers, my Irish clan, I stood apart and together, just as I stood apart and together with my father all my life, a treacherous child of his exile.

I also grew up in the stone streets of a city of half a million strangers, a world away from this ancient land. Another creature. In the city I studied philosophy at an old university; my teachers rightly taught me to question the appearances of all things. I lived and worked in a land of words, urban strangers, tall buildings and blocked-out horizons. The tools in my hands were notebooks, pens and keyboards, not the hammers, chisels and shovels the islanders used to gouge at the soil. I was far from the sight of the earth, the burl of the wind on your face, the snatch of a car door in a gale and the sound of a shore. I lived in the surrounding of foreign lives, meshed in the gyre of descending plane engines, the fractious meld of traffic, the recoil of sirens somewhere in the night and the star blinding wall of street lamps. The noise of the world, the pavement echo of stranger's words, was as different as it could possibly be from Dookinella.

In Dookinella, I was struggling to understand what the watchers saw or wanted in Sonny's death. How could these relative strangers relieve the burden of these agonies? What need for this public stage? I wanted the watchers to go away and leave Sonny's dying alone. But it was all too late. Sonny's wake, long before his death, had already begun. And we – my dying father, brothers and sisters, and the watchers – were being swept forward within these ancient rituals. The days that followed would forever change my understanding of the meaning of life, and my own death.

How do we become the people we are? The mystery of our lives. Born within the slipstream of our father's and mother's lives, we follow involuntarily in their wake. We never fully grasp the unseen currents that shift and shape; the imprint of their fathers and mothers before; the rites and cultural rituals of the preordained path; marriage, position, children; the flaws and inevitable failures of the mortal road. The onrush of our own lives, the glare of present novelty, blinds us. How much do we just re-enact variants of our forebears' script? Mumble out the words of the same life song. By the time we believe we have seized command of our destiny we are already forged, unconsciously repeating determined patterns. Or torn by the rupture, as I was, between the city and an older, more tribal identity. In the becoming of our selves, in the confusion of the city, the mass of others around us, we think we escape the chain of lives behind us. But we never do. The baggage is invisibly passed on, transmuted into other forms, reappearing in other guises down the line; the trail of a wave, our own inexplicable response erupting somewhere within our futures. The wake of the past, our past, is always with us.

Hail Mary, full of grace . . .

I stayed silent in the song of voices. But, as we slipped into the final decade of the rosary, the grip of my past overtook me; I began to pray too. Doctors say hearing is the last sense of a dying animal so perhaps even in Sonny's coma the sound of the rosary was a comfort – familiar voices, familiar prayers. We were singing out to Sonny, soothing him as though he were a child. A lullaby as he was falling, falling. Cradling him into death. Perhaps Sonny was beyond caring. But for us, the watchers, this keen was a sustaining ritual to control our fear, affirm our beating hearts and contain our sadness at his passage out.

. . . the Lord is with thee . . .

Involuntarily I prayed for Sonny, my father. I prayed hard for death to overtake him, this agony to end. And selfishly I prayed for myself.

Holy Mary, Mother of God, pray for me now and at the hour of my death.

The final verses ended. The voices of the chorus of watchers tapered into silence, and confusion.

Huh, Huh . . .

Sonny was still breathing. We listened on in the fractured stillness.

Huh, huh, huh.

The emaciated body would not stop. By the bedside Aunt Tilda, whose grandmother Mariah had been a *bean chaointe* for decades, seemed thrown by the failure of her prediction. Tilda reached out for a pulse on the paper skin of Sonny's withered left arm. It was faint; Sonny was alive. The frenetic breathing . . . *huh . . . huh* . . . dipped then slowed to an even rhythm. We would have to wait for death a little longer.

The gathering broke apart. We came back into our separate selves, awkwardly embarrassed now by our present intimacy. The room was far too crowded, too close. I struggled to find a language, the words, for what had just passed between the watchers. And what

I felt. Outside, dawn had come unnoticed and it was already as light as midday, though it was still five in the morning. My younger sister, Teresa, exhausted by the long vigil and the recent birth of her second child, went straight back to bed. A few watchers joined Aunt Tilda in the kitchen for tea and talk of other dyings. Cousin Bernadette volunteered to sit vigil with Sonny for the next hour. Sonny in his death coma, even more so than his newest born grandchild, was never now to be left alone.

I slipped away out the front door and down the road to the ocean. The beach at Dookinella runs for three miles in a long crescent from the base of Minaun to the local town with its two bars, a butcher, a post office and a shop. The beach has no real name. The islanders call it 'the strand' or 'back the shore'. The eastern end of the strand begins in the wild sea coves of Minaun, cut off at high tide, untouched and unaltered by man, where jagged cliffs fall hundreds of feet sheer into the surging tide. Beyond the coves lies the beach, shaped by eternal waning and waxing tides and ever shifting sands and stones.

The island is old, older than human time, dating long before the fossil era, the bedrock 590 million years old. The ocean, ice ages, the wind, the earth and time have created this place rather than any living thing. The cliffs of Minaun have been falling, piece by piece, into the ocean for hundreds of millions of years. And for the same number of years the ocean has been smashing, churning and breaking each rock fall, pulverising vast angular slabs into mere grains of sand. Ice ages, too, have carried their glacial till, a random debris of red and green sandstones, quartz and granites, out to sea, down the coast for hundreds of miles, and then back onto land to be pounded and polished in a million tides. Together the tide, waves and wind have swept their harvest onto shore creating a huge natural embankment of rounded beach stone – most no bigger than your fist – seven metres high and three miles long; a measureless shingle rampart. There are hundreds of millions and millions of beach rocks, even billions; without them half the island would be under the water.

The ocean never ceases the assault of creation and destruction. At every high tide, Atlantic breakers smash down on these mounds of stone. The retreating waters then shush back to sea through now vibrating rocks just before the next incoming wave renews the onslaught. Even on a still dawn you hear the clap, boom and roar of the thudding waters break on the shoreline. If there was no one left on the planet, the indifferent surge would go on waxing and waning. Twice a day, ever since the Moon was captured by Earth's gravity, and the oceans rose, every tide carves out a new line of struggle, a different wave pattern in the rocks; but the vastness of the rampart, the countless individual stones together, absorbs the wild ocean's energy.

Fresh waters, too, flow down from the hills into the ocean, dribbling out through the embankment of stones forming mini canyons in the sands of the strand before every snaking channel is obliterated again by the incoming tide.

The sands themselves flow west, then east. Out and in. Draining away into the ocean to expose the violent tilted bedrock of the earth. And then surging back, covering over nature's tumult, replenishing the strand again in no discernible pattern. Erosional tides suck sand and stone out to sea. Depositional tides recycle sands and stone back to shore. The shoreline never breaks.

Down on the beach you are most often alone; just you, the far horizon and the twin oceans of sky and sea. The wind sings in the air. Whipping sand strings flare out across the flat expanse and the solitary track of your feet runs back as if into infinity. It is hard not to feel small in the force of this place. Or even remember the worries of the city life you left behind.

Dookinella is a dangerous edge of the world. The power of the scourging tide is rewritten in ever-changing stone patterns on the rampart embankment twice daily. Offshore, there is a strong rip current that deters most swimmers and surfers. Beyond the rip there is America, 3,000 miles away. The water is cold and the green Atlantic breakers, unimpeded from the deep ocean, can easily knock you off your feet. Wave after wave engulfs you as the rip tide sucks hard at the sand beneath your feet. At first everything in the water is uncertain, scary: the dangers too wild. But if you hold your place, steel yourself in the moment, the fear lessens; the glistening waters lose their threat, and you can plunge headlong, surfing into the waves, whooping in delight, embracing the elements.

Sonny never lost his wonder for the ocean, going shoring and hunting the high-water mark for the flotsam and jetsam of the tide. Along its mark, strange treasures are scattered, bleached out in the light like relics: fluorescent orange fisherman's gloves, unscathed glass bottles, lost quill pen seagull feathers, skeins of fishing nets, lone running shoes, battered fishing crates, floats, clear plastic water bottles, suntan lotion sprays bearing Cyrillic script dumped overboard by distant ships, the odd eye-pecked body of a dead sheep, a porpoise or a seal, cast-off rope and driftwood timber.

Different seasons bring different harvests. In high summer, blooms of purple moon jellyfish and their stinging compass jellyfish cousins are carried to shore. Thousands of translucent floating blue sailors, small hydrozoans that drift on the ocean surface, lie marooned at low tide. Turbulent spring tides deposit forests of ocean-ripped brown kelp. Autumnal mysteries, colonies of percebes – gooseneck barnacles, a rare delicacy that sells for hundreds of pounds a kilo in the city – arrive on encrusted wooden logs. With every high tide the ocean adds or subtracts from its jetsam until a big storm hits; the waves swallow everything, and the beach is stripped back to stone.

The tide's driftwood – storm-tossed, wind-wracked, salt-scorched – is fantastically shaped; burnished mahogany, dark pine, silvery bark-stripped logs and dismembered wooden chests. Often, the tidal haul is part of some former thing; embedded with nails and bolts that drove the wreckage's original purpose. The ocean delivers nature's cast-offs too; tree trunks, clumps of dried cliff heather and limbs of ancient bog wood somehow washed to sea. If the driftwood has been in the water for any length of time it will be hollowed out, eaten through by the fearsome *Teredo navalis*, the naval worm that burrows its way into wooden hull sailing ships.

When the wind blows onshore there is often enough wood for a whole day's fire. Sonny would gather the wood, wrapping bundles in scraps of fishing nets and dragging it home to let it dry out on the grate. Some pieces, set up on either side of the fire, seemed too beautiful to burn. But wood, sea and time are a destructive combination; the ocean's salt leaches out the wood's natural protective oils. As the timber dries, it loses the ocean's sheening lustre and turns dull grey. In the fire, the driftwood burns with a crackling, spurting fury until everything is consumed; the ash in the morning is fine. All that remains are twisted iron nails – the last link to a lost purpose.

A few days before this final gathering, Sonny had risen from his deathbed for his last sight of the great ocean. Teresa drove him down to the end of the road, to the base of Minaun and the perpetual stream of *Abhainn Mór*, where in dry summers he had gathered water as a child and carried it in buckets back three quarters of a mile to the village. Someone took a picture of them there. Sonny, gaunt and frail, can barely stand and is leaning against the side of the car for support. He is smiling. My sister is smiling, too, triumphant that this journey proved possible.

Down on shore on that milky morning, I knew Sonny would never return. His next journey would be in a coffin to the graveyard on a nearby mountain, hidden in the mist, where all our ancestors lay buried. On the beach the tide was out and I slowly descended down the rampart of stones into the enclosing mist. On the strand, within a few steps, I was fogged in, directionless. Blinded. I felt as if I was submerged; the only sound the whispers of far off waves. At the ocean's edge, thin skeins of water lapped the sand, leaving a trail of bubbles behind that floated and then burst. The tide was waning, draining away into the limitless ocean, mixing salt and fresh with the waters of the mountain running out on the beach. The flowing mountain waters had carved out their own small seas in the deep sand, some of which had become cut off from the receding tide. In the mist it was easy to lose your footing and plunge knee-deep, sinking into quicksand, a chilly incoming wave surging around your legs. Unsure of the danger, my trousers sodden to the thigh, I turned back from the water's edge to rejoin the living, the dying and my father's wake.

WHISPERS

Death is a whisper in the Anglo-Saxon world.

Instinctively we feel we should dim the lights, lower our voices and draw the screens. We want to give the dead, the dying, the grieving, room. We say we do so because we don't want to intrude. And that is true.

What could we say anyway?

Hi, how do you feel about soon being dead?

Supposing no one has told them they are dying? Or they don't want to know?

Whatever you do don't even mention the word 'cancer'.

Or 'dying'.

You would only upset them. Who wants to talk about their own death? Who wants to talk about death at all?

But what else could you possibly talk about?

The weather?

Their holidays? Football? What?

It would all be too awkward. What can you even say to the bereaved?

Did she say anything at the end?

What was it like in the hospital room when he . . . passed?

Did you see her?

Was there a smell?

Morbid.

Uncomfortable.

For everyone.

Embarrassing. People would think you were weird.

Of course, it is not just the pain and anguish of others that deters us. We don't want to see the sick, smell the decay of wizened flesh, feel the coldness of the corpse, or hear the cry of keening women. We don't want to intrude on the dying because we don't want to look at the mirror of our own death.

Why have we lost our way with death?

How can it be possible to never talk out loud about death in a world where everyone dies?

There is no great secret that must continue to be closely held for fear of its disclosure. No revelation to be unveiled. No accident nor tragedy, no futile contest nor wrong, not played out a hundred thousand times before; at sea, in foreign fields, a hospital ward, in a street, in war, on a toilet, by cancer, at the gates of Troy, in victory or defeat, in madness or massacre, with or without purpose, amidst your tomatoes, by heart attack, after a long and painful illness, suddenly by your own hand, in the company of strangers, or at home alone in your own bed. Lovers lost, husbands gone, comrades killed, beloved children untimely ripped or aged parent laid to rest.

Death is terrifyingly ordinary. It happens to

everyone, everywhere, sometime. Worse of all there are no medical deferments out of it, no credit default swaps, no underhand bargains to be struck. There are no 'disruptive' mortality apps. If you breathe, you die.

And there's nothing new to say or write about death – not since the ancient Greeks and Homer's *Iliad* – except that, for the last two centuries, Western society has slowly striven and largely succeeded in removing the dead and dying from public sight. We have pulled the curtains across, privatised our mortality and turned death into a whisper.

Officially, the deceased have become obscene. In the United Kingdom it is a criminal offence to outrage public decency by exposing a corpse near a public highway. In the United States, embalming the dead is deemed a public health necessity. The path to the grave is therefore determined by a professional 'death industry' who hold Las Vegas conventions and date their 'mortality co-workers' on subterranean internet sites. Death in the West is a closed door on a closed room in a closed world.

If we are asked, most of us say we would like to die at home surrounded by those we love. Statistics show the reverse; the majority of us will end our lives on a general hospital ward strapped into various machines, sedated down to delirium, being industrially shuffled off by what has become our Western Death Machine. Corralling the sick away from public view and discreetly disposing of their bodies is the unvoiced mission of every Western hospital. Whether in a private room or on a crowded ward behind hastily drawn bed curtains, death is sequestered, redefined as medical failure and a shameful public embarrassment.

We have come to believe that this medical undertaking is our natural order. That the old and the sick will die happier amidst the babbling noise and alien light of a hospital ward. That the indignities inflicted upon them are necessary because a 'home death' – all those fluids, faeces, corruption – is too overwhelming. And that being packed off in the ambulance to die amongst strangers – whoever happens to be on that night's hospital shift – is what the dying deserve, because this is how life now ends, for all of us.

Like magic, our Western Death Machine can make the dead disappear. Once they stop breathing, the newly deceased slip away sight unseen into a nether world of cunningly disguised solid-sided trolleys, forbidding mortuaries and closed coffins. Most families never see their dead because, as we all know, or have at least been told by someone, somewhere, even if we can't exactly remember when, that the minute someone dies their rotting body is so full of horrible diseases like Ebola and their corpse would kill you just by touching them.

Or maybe you could catch something, your own death, just by being in the same room?

Why would you want to look anyway?

We console ourselves with morally crippling clichés.

Isn't it best to remember them as they really were?

Instead of the waxwork off the set of *Psycho* we are sure, sight unseen, they have instantly become. But unless we do see our dead how will we ever truly know?

If your father, mother or lover were not incarnate in flesh and blood, with an average daily temperature of 37° Celsius, in the same flesh that now lies cold and flaccid on the mortuary slab, who was this other bodiless 'them' thing that you are remembering instead? The 'them' you never met?

Your mother might cease to be but her physical body never ceases to be the dead her. And if you loved your mother in life then surely it is only natural that you would love and respect her body in death, and see and touch her flesh?

In the Western Death Machine, those who view their dead – like voyagers to strange unknown lands – are said to be exceptional. Brave. Most adult Westerners have never seen or touched a human corpse.

Have you?

One?

Two?

Count off the real dead bodies you have seen on your fingers?

If the dead and the sun are life's constants, how can the sight of the deceased be so rare you can count the cadavers you've seen on one hand?

*

Wouldn't you, we, just be horrified if No. 22, up the road, in defiance of the *proper* regulations, took their dead mother home from the hospital, laid her out on show in the front room for a few days and invited all the neighbours, and their kids, round to have a look? What if they served tea and sandwiches?

What about the public hygiene? Surely there must be some sort of rule against that sort of thing?

And how ridiculous would it be if the men from Nos 28, 32, 36 and 44 said they would feel privileged to dig your mother's grave by hand themselves, and wouldn't take any money? Or just enough for a few pints each at the Crossroads Inn?

What would you think if every uncle or brother you had, every male in your family, and failing that even the old men in your mother's golf club, came round en masse and said it was their duty and fervent wish to carry your mother's coffin on their shoulders to the grave? Out of respect for their mortal sister. And that it would be one of life's greatest honours if you allowed them to so do so?

Or if the whole neighbourhood, your colleagues from work, plus a few more strangers who you've never met, insisted on coming to her funeral? Uninvited. Just showed up. If they further insisted, each and every one of them, of lining up to shake your hand at the open grave. And what if they then said the same dull cliché over and over again – about how sad they felt about her death? And if for the next few months other people who knew you, and sometimes strangers who didn't, kept on accosting you? In the supermarket, the office, the bar, to say they too were sorry about the loss of your mother?

Would those repeated public expressions of concern – of grief and mourning – be the most terrible thing in the world?

Death in the West comes to us as news from a foreign land. A country only the intrepid visit. It is a happening elsewhere, over the horizon, like the distant wars, airplane accidents, mass shootings by masked madmen – earthquakes and disasters that fill the evening news. Or sometimes, in the shock of the fall of the great: an assassination of a politician; another drug-drowned film star or a random massacre. Even then we flinch. The dead, indifferent to further harm or shame, can never be openly shown. They must be covered over with tablecloths, body bagged or pixelated out. We protect ourselves on the grounds of public decency, lest sight of mortal flesh disturb our innocence, or puncture our deathless world. We have a taboo about saying the D word out loud. So we dissemble with a hundred and more euphemisms about 'passing', substituting transitive verbs for the noun, dead, and the intransigent state of deadness.

We censor our children from the knowledge that one day Mr Death, our Mortal Bogeyman, is going to get them. Who would ever take a child to a funeral? Or dream of letting them touch a corpse? The thought alone is *sick*. Even in all the fake mayhem and killing in the movies we find it hard to say the 'D' word. Hollywood heroes never die on board alien spacecraft – they just don't make it back. Fictitious corpses are always shrouded, even though it is just actors pretending to be dead. There are complicated Movie Land rules about the colours and precise quantities of fake blood, red or blue, shown on screen – lest death appears too vivid, too real.

We blank death out in the Western Death Machine. Walk into any newsagent and scan the rows of glossy magazines, fashion, biographies of the thin personalities of so-called celebrities, hardwares, softwares, music, movies and hobbies. You'd think in all this selling of seeming newness and eager capitalism there might be space for a few constant titles: *Your Coming Death!* or *Death Rites Revisited*. Why isn't there a FixUpYour Funeral.com comparative website for squeezing the best deal on caskets, grave locations, cremations and the catering? Or a UberHearse app to get the best rates to the nearest graveyard? How about a YourDeathDay app on your smartphone to chart your heartrate and fitness regime alongside your likely actuarial run? A wrist-worn countdown clock, calibrated with your birth year, daily aerobic exercise rate, calorific intake and linked with your genetic inheritance in terms of the death ages of your grandparents and parents, and annual income, to see if you are pushing your projected death date closer or further along?

Strangely, there's no place in our mortal market for a death guide.

School boards tediously agonise over sex education – what age, where and when, penises and vaginas, AIDS and STDs, sexual etiquette – but as far as I know not one of them ever sets down a curriculum hour of mortality studies.

Why not?

Reading these sentences or talking about dying is not going to kill you, and death is so utterly predictable it's easy to do the existential arithmetic. Given current Western life expectancies, most of us, statistically at least, will die in our early eighties.

Take your birth year, add eighty, and do the sums.

$1940 + 80 = 2020$

$1951 + 80 = 2031$

$1962 + 80 = 2042$

$1973 + 80 = 2053$

$1984 + 80 = 2064$

$1995 + 80 = 2075.$

And so on.

Get out a pencil and write your projected expiry date down here on the page.

If you don't have a pencil handy you could always use a pen?

Your personal death date. The end point for You.

Have you ever known the date before?

Isn't it strange that we don't ever want to work out what being mortal means?

Or ask the question?

And these few sentences, in this book, might be the first time in your whole life you have ever written down your actuarial death date? Or thought about it? Does the date seem chilling? Even on paper? Like those French gravestones where the name and birth year, but not the death year, of the future occupant is already economically chiselled on the awaiting tomb.

Did you actually write the date down?

Or are you not going to write the date down because it's just a gimmick in a book?

Or bad luck?

Or because you really don't want to?

Don't want to what though?

Write it down?

Or die?

The thing is that none of the above so-called reasons for not writing your actuarial death date down are really reasons at all. They are just denials and fears.

Here is another space to have a go.

Of course, we could argue about the exact year – at the front or at the far end of your particular death decade – taking into account complex weighted epidemiological calculations connected to your wealth, genetic heritage, locality, diet and social class. Your use, abuse or non-use of stimulants; tobacco, alcohol, opiates, cannabis and other drugs. Your daily exercise schedule. But we would just be quibbling.

All the money and power in the world won't alter the final outcome; the worst of tyrants, the richest of bankers, the billionaires of Silicon Valley, all die too. That there will be a death date, four score and something maybe, is the important thing. Your hours run.

Of course not everyone makes it to eighty. Fate can deal a vicious blind hand and from nought to thirty you could be dead of some rare childhood cancer, heart defect or taking a bullet for being in the right place at the right time in the wrong neighbourhood.

After thirty, earlier in some cases, we all get to play around with our own death date. Add on the pounds, drink, do drugs, smoke, a bit of recklessness with guns and cars, poverty or cancer, and the date drops through the floor by decades or more.

The Unlucky You.

Knock off five years each for your drink, weight and druggie negatives and write out your new projected death date down here.

I know you might want to fiddle the figures but lying now to yourself, or in your diminished future, won't alter the outcome.

Who knows? Life is unpredictable. Perhaps you'll pick up some horrible infection: meningitis, cerebral malaria or tuberculosis. Maybe the Celestial Sniper will decide to take you out with a side-swiping truck, the traffic lights on green. What about a simple trip, a fatal misstep, in the domestic war zone?

That tumble from the step, the one you never saw, and crack to the head on the backstairs at work/the basement/disco/the holiday pool/the sidewalk outside, which ended in the brain haemorrhage that ended you.

Or the day in the shower when you first feel the 'pea' in your breast. The 'pea' that blossoms on the fruit metaphor cancer scale into an 'apricot' or 'plum' lump that morphs again into a 'melon'-sized unkillable cancer, no matter how many times the doctors slash away, burn your flesh or run chemo poison through your veins.

How about the other sly, life-ender dodge of getting on the wrong plane?

What if the Hand of God decides to choke you to death on your next portion of Parma ham?

Or you could, like the Queen of England, defy all expectations and reign longer than anyone ever expected. Live long and win the Great Genetic Lottery.

The Lucky You.

Until the day your luck runs out and you die like everyone else.

Here is a rough marker to help with the probabilities. In the United States, 0.0173 per cent of Americans make it past a hundred: 55,000 out of a population of 320,000,000. In the UK, the figure is 0.02 per cent or 14,450 out of a population of 65,000,000. Long odds.

It's a lot worse if you are male. Only one in five centenarians is male; there are fewer than 3,000 100-year-old men in the current UK population and just 11,000 male centenarians in the United States. A ratio of one 100-year-old man per 22,491 other citizens in the UK and 1:29,090 citizens in the United States.

One way to think about these odds is to calculate how many spectators would have to die before the English national football team could field a full squad of eleven male centenarians at Wembley Stadium in London, capacity 90,000. The stadium would have to fill, empty, fill, empty, and then fill two thirds again to reach the 247,401 other humans statistically required before our aged survivor squad take to the pitch. The ratio for female centenarians is more favourable 1:5,622 vis-a-vis the general population. So it would only take 61,000 other dead people in the stands before a female squad of centenarians ran onto the turf. But the odds for any one woman are still over a 1:5,000 chance.

Even if you are going to be that lucky 1:5,000 female survivor, then it might be useful to start visualising, and mentally erasing, those other 4,999 dead people. They don't have to share your birthday but just be born around the same time, maybe the same year, or in the same class at school. You could start with your family, brothers and sisters, the other kids you knew at nursery, school, college, university or on the local football team. Then you could move on to your work-mates, neighbours, your Facebook friends, anyone else you ever knew on the internet, or maybe just strangers you see on the street who roughly look the same age.

How many faces, how many names, have you remembered? One hundred? Two hundred? But supposing your extended lifespan really did depend on you being able to name every classmate, friend, work colleague, you ever knew so they could die instead of you? And the winner was the person who remembered better and wrote down more names and got closer to 5,000? Or closer to 22,000–29,000 others if you are male? Do you still think you would win? Or that being the last survivor of your generation is really a blessing?

Are you going to be that Lucky?

Statisticians calculate that, by 2120, the proportion of centenarians will grow from 0.02 per cent to 1.6 per cent of the general population. Most of us, though, are not going to make it onto the Wembley pitch, but will meet our ordinary end somewhere amidst the milling spectators. And we have not yet started discussing how many of our 100-year-old soccer players have to be wheeled onto the pitch, and can neither play football nor walk, talk or think. Psychologically, you might be better off buying an actual lottery ticket.

Realistically, even if things go well, you might at best have another half decade on the actuarial average. Eighty plus five.

But would living that long even be Lucky? We might want to believe eighty is the new sixty, but biologically it remains eighty. Jogging another lap round the park, stocking up on juicers, Botox and plastic surgery, taking vitamin pills or hiring the best oncologist money can buy might possibly delay but will not stop your slow demise. Nor will your ending be either neat or quick. Living longer is not the same as living longer free of ailment. By our nature, we stagger step by step towards the grave one decrepitude at a time; bad knees, leaky hearts, wheezy lungs, arthritic fingers, bleeding brains, mutating DNA, flailing kidneys, cardiac arrests, failing sight, diabetes, clogged arteries, deafness and chronic pain. This mortal race will not be won, however long you intend to compete.

Nature has another trick, too. Even those who run furthest can still come in last. What if you became another Tithonus? Cursed with the gift of a perpetual but senile life after his nymph lover Eos asked for Zeus to make Tithonus immortal but failed to ask for eternal youth. Alive but absent. A living death in the wilderness of Alzheimer's. Another President Reagan?

Of course that won't happen to you either, with all your academic degrees, or those crossword puzzles you do to keep yourself mentally active. Except one in three eighty-five-year-olds has got Alzheimer's, and every old folks' home is already filled with the demented. The odds shorten again. Would your last self-conscious wish not be for a sooner, luckier, death?

How about a different date?

Death is a universal occurrence with two options; you can do death well or you can do death badly. You can encounter your own death and the death of those you love in terror, in denial, in confusion, in blind panic, in shocked surprise and in despair. Amazed, outraged, angry that this alien implacable stranger is erasing the Sovereign State of You out of existence just when you had all those other holiday plans booked. How can life be so unfair? Doesn't Azrael, the Archangel of Death, know who *you* are?

Or you could try the other option and learn how to die.

How to die? What sort of proposition is that? What kind of book is this?

Most how-to books, unless they have the honesty of sewing or car manuals, offer promises of material success; you will earn more, impress your boss, grow rich, and sleep with glamorous people. But not this one. Most of the time, those other books and their simplistic formulas, are part of the white noise we use to shut death out. To hide. Learning how to die is the very opposite. It is to come out from under those collar and tie disguises, your padded-shoulder business suit, the daily words of impurpose linked to what will turn out to be a largely vacuous quest to gain position three rungs further up the pecking order. It is to expose yourself to your own mortality and question the rationale of many of the common devices we employ to fool ourselves. The shiny glimmer of seeming newness and the shell of the outward appearance of hollow things. Our hours filled up with the sound of words, the flicker of inconsequent images, swiftly forgotten; the smell, once you recognise it, of your own superficial self. Or the glories of status, even marriage, which fleetingly last only as long as you can remember why you ever wanted them. To accept death is to question the value of many of those desires. To face the best of our fear instead and look up towards the far horizon.

The search for life meaning is not the purpose of this book, but thinking about your own mortality inevitably returns the questioner to another existential question.

Is this the life I wanted? Or still want?

Learning how to die will not make you richer or sexier or help you buy a bigger house or yacht. It will not chart out a plan to worldly success. Guarantee you contentment. Nor will this book. Humans are restless creatures and there is no one answer to the happiness question, only further desires and fears. Blissful joy usually has a one-hour time limit, and we all have separate needs, responsibilities and wants to fulfil. Your life, and the pursuit of whatever satisfies your hungers, remains your own responsibility. But so too is your death.

If it's any consolation, on the day when death comes none of the above will matter anyway. We will leave life as we entered it, in skin, bone, flesh and nothing else. All of us need to find a way to handle death. It will be a lot easier if we just copy what the Irish already do.

If you have never been to a real Irish Wake, and just watched the movie version, then you probably think a wake is just another Irish piss-up; a few maudlin drunks gathered around a coffin. But you would be mistaken.

The wake is the oldest rite of humanity, once practised in some form by every culture on earth, reaching back beyond the fall of Troy to our Neolithic ancestors and further still.

In the *Iliad*, the great eighth-century BCE epic poem that is a foundation work of Western civilisation, when the Trojan king Priam returns to Troy with the battered body of his dead son, Hector, the Trojan women rush into the streets to touch Hector's corpse. The women block the way. They keen and wail over Hector's dead body until Priam orders them to let him pass:

'Hereafter ye shall have your fill of wailing, when I have brought him unto his house.'

Hector is taken home, cleansed and laid out on his fretted marital bed. 'Minstrel leaders of the dirge, who wailed a mournful lay' are stationed by his corpse along with his mother Hekabe and Helen of Troy. His wife Andromache cradles his lifeless body and eulogises:

'Husband thou art gone young from life and leavest me a widow in thy halls. Our child is yet but a little one who I fear shall never grow to mankind but perish when this city is utterly destroyed.'

Hector is waked for nine days and then ritually burnt on the tenth, his funeral ending in a great feast. The last line of the *Iliad* ends: 'Thus held they funeral for Hector tamer of horses.'

Homer's description of Hector's wake, the keening women, the feasting and the funeral games, is still easily recognisable to any wake-goer on the island. A real wake has a real dead body and the sight and touch of a corpse, a dead one-of-us is both transcendent and tangible proof of the mortal limit of every human life; our common kinship.

A wake is the best guide to life you could ever have. To put it crudely, if we, as individuals, are the mortal hardware, then the wake is the software our forebears used on the rest of the network, a series of protocols and rites, to code death and communally survive the mortality of any one unit. An enacted How-to-Live-Beyond-Death manual, with some variants, to be shared out amongst the gathered mourners.

We are a lot more than hardware and software. Some instincts towards the dead are still hard-wired into us despite the blinding of the Western Death Machine. Respecting dead bodies, laying them properly to rest in burial, or through cremation, is part of our universal belief system whatever the religion or ideology. An act of humanity. The very word we use for a grave of human dead is inhumation.

In Homer's *Iliad*, the Gods castigate the great Greek champion Achilles for his abuse of his Trojan enemy Hector's body after their fight to the death before the gates of Troy. The desecration of Hector's body is an offence against nature. In our civilisation, we too believe we have a moral obligation to the bodies of our enemies. We are repulsed by those who in war desecrate the bodies of dead, cast their remains on the plains to be savaged by wild animals or bury their victims unmarked in mass graves. We define such actions as inhumane; of not being proper or natural.

More selfishly, physical contact with the dying, the dead and the bereaved is a kind of inoculation, a piece of armour to carry around with you in preparation for the moment when you personally need to deal with death.

Come to death? Learn how to die? Does it still seem impossible, nihilistic?

Suicidal even?

But suppose you thought death was like a marathon that one day you knew you had to run. Or you had to help other people – your family, people you love – run their marathons. And it was totally compulsory, no getting out of it. Nor was there to be any warning on when the race was called. You just had to drop whatever you were doing and start running the whole twenty-six miles that second. Now, instead of pretending it was never going to happen, don't you think it might be useful to get in a little practice beforehand? A few laps round the local park? A regular workout to keep in shape so you were ready for the day? The hour?

Well a wake is a bit like preparing for that death marathon, and even the training, whether you fumble and fail a few times, will make you not richer but wiser and more thoughtful. More human. The first step is to get started with a few practice laps early on. First on other people's deaths and then on your own. Just like my fathers and mothers have been doing on the island through the rite of the Irish Wake for the last few thousand years.

ORIGINS

Sonny was an ordinary man. He wasn't rich or powerful. He never built an empire, changed history or held public office. He knew the world would not be equal. His name never appeared in the newspapers and the world never paid him much attention, and Sonny knew the world never would. Nor are the exact details of his life important to this story. He was born poor in a remote Irish village, devoid of electricity, mains water and tarred roads, in much the same way the poor have been born in such places for most of human history. His boyhood was a constant round of drudgery; carrying buckets of water home from the waterfall of *Abhainn Mór* in dry summers, climbing Minaun to round up cows for milking or move sheep to pasture, cutting turf in the bogs in the spring, planting barley, gathering hay in the summer and digging potatoes in the small fields of Dookinella. His early life followed the seasons, the cycles of planting and harvests, the rites of births, marriages and deaths, which the islanders have followed forever. He was a clever child but his formal education was limited. Sonny did not get the chance to go to school for very long and had to teach himself almost everything he knew about machines, cars and construction.

Forced into exile and away from the island by poverty, Sonny worked most of his life as a construction foreman building roads; ordering other men around even though his natural shyness must have made the burden of this command difficult to bear. He lived in a city where men were builders, machine drivers, plumbers, electricians, and women, nurses, factory workers, shop girls, housewives, mothers and dinner ladies. He was uncomfortable giving speeches at weddings, didn't like wearing suits, eating in fancy restaurants or strange peppery foods.

Sonny was good with his hands, though, useful to have around if something went wrong with the electrics, the car, the drains, or if furniture needed to be moved. Sonny had an art with tools: chisels, hammers, saws, cables, fuse boxes, spades and shovels. He owned his own house and didn't believe the state, the repair company in a phone book or anyone else would save him. He got on with the doing by himself. He was a man of quiet responsibilities, slow to anger, who never faltered in his duties. He enjoyed the creation of things; hewing out a stone fireplace with his own hands, running an electric cable to a stable to light a workshop, or planting a garden. He was frugal, carefully husbanding any spare bit of wood, wire and building materials that came his way for future use. He knew the Latin names of plants and in the baggy right-hand pocket of his tweed jacket carried mini-secateurs to snip away in foreign gardens and clandestinely gather cuttings. He could play the bagpipes and the accordion, and had a strong melodious voice. He taught all his children to sing, too, by listening to what he called the *air* and singing along. In the 1960s he bought a 35mm camera, developed his own prints, ran a darkroom and also shot home movies on Super 8mm. Like a lot of people, Sonny had some talents he would never fully realise in life.

Sonny married when he was twenty-three. In the black-and-white wedding picture he stands proudly beside my mother against a background suggestive of a grand country house. But the illusion of a well-to-do landed couple, just leaving their spacious drawing room, frays away at the edges. In the picture they stand on ragged bits of different coloured carpet and the felt on the raised stage below their feet is ripped and torn. The stylised background is fake, the shot posed in the studio of a small town Irish photographer. My father's right hand hangs unnaturally down by his side as if he is unsure where to put it. This wedding picture is a rite of passage of the rural poor and the married young; a hopeful wish.

Sonny's face still has the look of a boy who has un-wittingly found himself top of the class and can't quite believe his luck. His ears are too big for his head. His hair is one massive brown crinkly, unruly wave that he always combed back. Even in death, fifty years later, with the colour turned silver grey, he held the same dense shock of hair. Beside him my mother, fresh faced, stands in a tweed jacket, pleated skirt and stockings. She is holding her white wedding gloves in her left hand and has her right arm cocked in my father's elbow. She looks more apprehensive, unsure of the fate they have determined upon just one hour before. Her jacket is tight with the growing child who hastened these nuptials. Their lives are all before them.

Sonny's marriage produced seven children. He devoted most of his days to supporting them and a good part of his nights to nursing his babies in the cot at the foot of his marital bed. Sixteen years separate the oldest and youngest of his children. He loved my mother, despite her erratic temper, and missed her badly when she died suddenly in her early sixties of a heart attack. He was lonely without her, a wounded creature bereft of comfort. Sonny was adrift, depressed and drew into himself. His loss, after their long marriage, diminished him. He came home from the city seeking sanctuary on the island, returning to Dookinella to share in another life with his youngest daughter, Teresa, newly married, his newest grandchild and son-in-law. He came home to live in the same house he had helped build as a child.

Sonny got a sheepdog pup and named him Darcy after his favourite childhood dog. Morning or evening, man and dog would trot off together to go shoring back the strand as he had done as a *gasúr*, a boy. Sonny filled his days with the hammering, building and planting. And he spent his nights visiting a whole clan of relations. He recovered.

Sonny was a very ordinary man and his life passed unnoticed by a wider world. But Sonny did have one advantage over most of us; he knew how to die. And he knew how to do that because his fathers and mothers on the island, wake after wake, had shown him how. They had trained Sonny all his life to die by giving a voice, a place, in their daily lives for the dying and the dead. And in showing Sonny how to die, those Irish fathers and mothers taught him other more important lessons. How to live. And how to love.

VOICES

On the island, death has a louder voice. Along with lonesome cowboys and weather reports of incoming Atlantic storms, the local country and western radio station runs a thrice-daily roll-call, seven days a week, of the freshly deceased – at 8 a.m., 10 a.m. and again at 5 p.m. The hour chimes, then a few, brief news headlines, a bit of solemn introductory music, and the announcer starts:

> The death has occurred of Noel Kearney of Ballyinclogher, Corraun. Peacefully at home after a short illness. Reposing at his residence. Removal of remains on Thursday at 6 p.m. to Our Lady Saviour church. Mass of the Resurrection at 10 a.m. Friday proceeding to interment at St Joseph's Cemetery.

There is a short pause and then the announcer continues, 'The death has occurred of Teresa Colbane . . .'

And on and on until the ten or so daily death notices are recited.

'The Deaths' are a big draw and the newly dead

also get their own page on the station's website. Other stations, elsewhere in Ireland, have a premium Deaths line, 95 cents a minute, just so you can check up on the recently departed. Listeners tune in to know who has died in their village, in the rest of Mayo, in the Connaught region, or in far-flung outposts of exile: Cleveland, Ohio; Los Angeles, California; Preston, England, Auckland, New Zealand.

Death on the island remains a very democratic activity. Going to see the dead as their body lies in a bed or a coffin in the front room, or at a funeral home, is part of life's pattern, a social obligation. An unremarked duty. Passing acquaintances, casual strangers, shake the hands of the bereaved family and offer their condolences. Sometimes politicians, hungry for votes, show up and work the crowd. Funerals are public events, a communal act of kinship. An affirmation that the life of the dead man or woman meant something, that they are no longer with us, and that it hurts us to lose them. More people can see you dead than you ever knew in life.

Most of the time the bereaved are glad you are there with them, too. No one checks your entitlement at the door or vets your emotional credentials at the church gate. Three hundred mourners will come to the funeral of an ordinary shepherd or farmer. The numbers for a retired teacher, a priest or a young suicide victim would be closer to a thousand. By the time an islander faces their own death in middle or later age they will have lost count of the sight of the dead and their funerals.

Strange as it might seem, the occurrence of death is a regular activity across the rest of the planet, too. In a good year, 1 per cent of the global population dies, 200,000 dead people a day, 73 million a year. An even spread. It's happening to someone in the street, the hospital, the town near you right now. Look up your city or town's population on the internet. Divide the figure by a hundred and you've roughly got the local annual death toll. In all the cities I have lived, half a million, a million, 8.5 million, the dead every year have occurred in far greater numbers than the island's entire population; 5,000, 10,000, 85,000. In London or New York, the radio announcer would have to read out, three times a day . . . *the death has occurred* . . . 230 times just to keep up. But you would never know.

In the city, I never heard dead strangers' names read out on the radio. Or my neighbours say they were just popping over to a wake house for a few hours this afternoon to avoid the early evening *rush* of mourners. Or anyone offer to sit awake through the long hours of night on a hard chair to guard a soul's safe passage to the afterlife. And return again another time in the dew of morning, as translucent spider webs glisten in the yellow flowering gorse, for the closing of a neighbour's coffin. And still go even though that deceased neighbour was a hard, embittered man who in petty disputes rankled over land, sheep and fences. Nor in city streets did I hear anyone softly sing out prayers for such a troubled soul – that Lazarus, the angels, saints and Jesus Christ himself would welcome him in death into the eternal Holy City of Jerusalem. And in that fabled resurrection find a peace which always eluded him in this earthly life. And that his trespasses, if not forgotten, will for the immediate comfort of his relatives be glided over until a more appropriate time of reckoning.

Nor in the city did I see anyone stand in the soft light of evening in a deceased woman's front garden, amidst the fuchsia and pampas grass, with fifty other mortals, to witness the removal of the remains. To watch as the pine coffin is carried out the front door and then perched on two household chairs on the green lawn, as the walls of the house are splashed and blessed with Holy Water from a recycled lemonade bottle. And then join in the final prayers before bearing witness to her coffin being lifted into the hearse and the chairs kicked over to mark an irreversible rupture between the living and the dead. An ancient death ritual that an anthropologist, if he or she happened to be passing, would define as a specific rite of reversal. The creation of an impenetrable barrier between the natural and spirit world to ensure the dead woman's soul can now never return inside the house to disturb the living. A pagan belief. Though, if you asked, no one in the crowd would know what the anthropologist was talking about. They would just tell you they were there in the garden to support their neighbours in this hour of need. As this is the sort of decent thing people do for the dead around here. Or have done for at least as long as they, or anyone, can remember.

In the city I never met anyone who drove up Maun, a long slow hill on the island that overlooks four villages, or anywhere like it, at six in the evening to wait by the side of the road for an incoming sixty-car funeral cortege accompanying the latest dead woman's coffin – who arrived from England on the Luton–Knock flight that same afternoon. Waiting for her coffin and hearse and the long tail of mourners' cars behind to pass on the narrow road and then, out of respect for the dead, join at the rear. To journey with her for the last couple of miles to the drab pebble dash Our Lady of the Assumption church at the Dookinella crossroads where she'll rest for the night. Even though with her being dead she'll never be able to thank you for the time, the petrol or your efforts. And to go to her Funeral Mass the next morning, whatever the weather, though you weren't that close since she lived away for so long; and you didn't know the family well either. But wasn't it heart-breaking for her to die so young of cancer, just thirty-nine, and her daughters still in their early teens? And after her Funeral Mass go to the graveyard for her burial on Slievemore mountain. Waiting in line by the cut grave in a field of headstones, the rain lashing with vengeance off the mountain, to shake the stung red hands of her bereaved husband, and her still stunned teenage daughters. Waiting to offer a sparse, well-worn phrase of comfort.

Sorry for your trouble.

Standing together in the deluge on this green mountain overlooking the great ocean, beside them now, in death, in these, the worst moments of their young lives. Perhaps the worst moments of their whole lives. Because surely what else could you do?

And if such unselfish concern for stricken strangers, a reaching out to dress another's wound, such acts of selfless loving compassion, are not the best of us, then it's hard to know what more could be asked of any other mortal soul. For in that act of open recognition at the wake, the removal and the grave, the mourner cannot but affirm to the bereaved, and bereaved to mourner, not the difference but the commonality of all human flesh.

If we can recognise each other as in some way equal at the grave, perhaps we can then, too, in other places, also see each other as the same creatures who have wants and needs and desires like our own. And so have more understanding of both our and their own frailties, and no longer divide ourselves into defining categories like rich or poor, city or islander, strong or weak, clever or stupid, but just human. All too human. Like us.

Even the words 'the death has occurred' spoken out loud on a country and western Irish local radio station are an act of revelation in the Anglo-Saxon world. A bigger shock still would be to discover another country where the dead, the living and the bereaved still openly share a world together beyond the denial of the Western Death Machine.

Death for sure is not a whisper on the island.

UNRAVELLINGS

I must have been nine that summer, a *gasúr*, and the world was unravelling. The Great Irish Emigration of the 1960s was sweeping everything away. The whole village of Dookinella had emptied down to just a handful of households, as hundreds of islanders fled for the boats to England or America, abandoning their lands, their homes, their families, and flowing into exile. Men, like tractors, were already a rarity. Each husband, each son, long gone, working on the building sites of England, or in America, sending money back home. Every house that remained relied on wages from another country. Our family home in Dookinella had fallen into limbo, shuttered, abandoned to spiders and window frame-devouring wood lice.

Out the back in the yard, like a marker tomb, was the rough breeze-block shed where the last family male, my Uncle John, had earned a half-living slaughtering sheep and driving round the island selling the hacked carcass from the boot of his Morris van on a flattened cardboard box. Even this primitive butchery did not pay. And then John too was on the boat, with his family, for a job on the railways in England. With Uncle John gone, grandfather Patrick was forced to go live with his daughter, my Aunt Mary, in the neighbouring village of Cabaun. With all the rest of his children in exile, scattered, seventy-nine-year-old Pat was too weak to look after himself, never mind his three cows, donkey, chickens, the semi-wild cats and Glen, his dog. He refused to budge until Aunt Mary came over and drove his cows to Cabaun. A few days later old Pat followed, packing his chickens and possessions into his donkey cart, intending only to stay for the winter. Glen, after several returns to Dookinella and enforced removals back to Cabaun, even more reluctantly settled into the exodus.

After two centuries, our time in Dookinella was over. The ocean foreshore at Dookinella was the one and only place from where our small clan sprang, and grandfather was the last of us, the last Toolis. We were finished, gone, died out. Lost.

As the winters passed, grandfather's house began to slide into decay. Rain ran down inside the chimneys. Great splodges of damp appeared in living room walls. Leaks sprung in roofs. Soot gushed from the chimney grate. Plaster fell in clumps from ceilings and walls. Cobwebs grew, flies buzzed and died on window sills and woodworm riddled the remaining furniture. The porch door swelled – or the frame shrank – the key grew rusty, and even unlocked you had to heave the door off its failed hinges to enter the musty interior.

Soon the house was no longer habitable; the roof another few winters away from collapsing in on itself.

Not everything was gone. Beyond the house was
a sprawl of sheds and little fields that still had their
uses. Turf, also known as peat, cut by hand from the
bogs in spring and used for fuel, could still be stored
against winter's rain in grandfather's once prized red
corrugated-iron Dutch barn. And so too could the hay
from the surrounding fields, to help feed Aunt Mary's
now enlarged cattle herd in the winters that lay ahead.
So every summer, adults and children, Aunt Mary,
Mother, Sonny and grandfather Pat himself came back
as day trippers in the donkey cart from Cabaun. We'd
gather in the hay and use the wreck of Dookinella as a
temporary work camp.

There is nothing romantic about peasant labour. Hay
making is akin to cleaning a large football field with
a dustpan and brush; raking and turning the wet cut
grass in the fields with a wooden, toothed hay rake from
ten in the morning until eight at night. Returning the
next day for another ten hours to shake and loosen the
same rolled-up carpet-like grass sheaves with a pitch-
fork into a drying wind. Then returning once again for
the final ten-hour session, to gather the hay in and build
the nursery rhyme haystacks we called tramcocks. If it
rained before the hay was securely gathered and pro-
tected in a covered tramcock, the whole process would
begin again.

After milking her Cabaun cows, feeding dogs, chickens and children, Aunt Mary loaded up the donkey cart and soon we were heading over to Dookinella, the cart bolting and juddering its way on the gravel road. When we got to the house, we children ran to the barred porch door, excited to be back again at this gigantic playhouse. From underneath the secret hiding place, an adjacent stone next to the door, Aunt Mary produced the long black key and turned the lock. We heaved at the door and stumbled into the dry stale porch antechamber before pushing on inside.

Grandfather's house remained caught in its moment of abandonment. There were tables, tablecloths, dusty wooden chairs, buckets of rusty nails, iron bedsteads, a statue of Jesus as the Child of Prague on the mantelpiece and a fading portrait of two popes and a beaming President John F. Kennedy high on the wall. In a back room we always called Uncle Jack's – even though he was long dead – a rasping file and a hammer lay on top of a painted and repainted dresser, whose drawers were stuffed with life's bric-a-brac: old spectacles, tickets for the labourer's boat back from England, twine, dried out tins of Vaseline and snuff, needles, odd buttons and decayed nine-volt radio batteries. Under the springs of Uncle Jack's bed, as if awaiting his return, were boxes of carpenter tools in wooden crates like last relics. Dookinella was an inventory of the spiralling disorder of exile; possessions too bulky, too useless to carry away, or simply overlooked at the last moment of departure.

In search of salvage, we children rifled in kitchen drawers for penknives, broken watches, objects whose purposes – like their owners' lives – had evaporated. In the scatter of outbuildings beyond the house, we pulled and wrenched at long-jammed shed-door bolts to discover blunt scythes hanging from the rotting rafters and boxes of strange tools used for purposes unknown. We hammered battered chisels into rock-hard, unused and now worthless bags of cement to see if we could make stone dissolve back to powder. We played hide and seek inside the empty piggery or took turns driving Uncle John's windowless, rear-axle-less Morris butcher's van, now lopsidedly moored forever in amongst the nettles in a back haggard. We clambered inside the timbers of the horseless cart and pulled at the redundant collars and bridles abandoned in the corner. We ignored stern warnings and mounted the rotten wooden outside staircase that led to the equally rotten roof timbers of the upstairs' granary to 'rescue' our neighbour Martin MacMonaghan's cat and her litter. We slid down mounted tramcocks and dived into the sea of hay now being gathered in the barn, and generally had a great time getting in the way. Somewhere in the midst of all the fun I also did a few stints as donkey driver.

I may have been nine, but every hand was still useful

in the relentless hours of hay making that filled the adults' days. I was conscripted and put in charge of the donkey and cart – the donkey boy – as Teresa, and cousins Michael and Ellen, played amongst or hindered the hay makers. My job was to lead the animal from field to barn and back as the cart it pulled was loaded and unloaded with hay. I held tightly on the halter and reins to stop the animal wandering away.

At the end of that long day, with the freshly gathered hay safe in the Dutch barn behind us, Sonny pulled out his brown leather-cased 35mm German camera and took a picture of us children next to the donkey cart. We pose hesitantly, close to the now silent breeze-block slaughterhouse. I am holding the animal's bridle, alongside six-year-old Teresa, supposedly in charge but inwardly frightened of being bitten by the donkey's snapping yellow piano key teeth. I am half-turned towards the camera, warily following Sonny's instructions, with my five-year-old cousin, Ellen, in the foreground. Cousin Michael sits behind on the make-shift wooden cart whose axle and wheels must have come from Uncle John's long-dead Morris. None of us is smiling. The sun has dipped behind clouds and the evening turned swiftly cold.

This picture taking is one last chore pressganged upon us in the final minutes as we pack up to go. Dressed in our wellingtons and jumpers, wrapped up against the evening's chill, we all are tired and bored of the long day's adventures. We want to be in the warmth of Aunt Mary's back kitchen in Cabaun; fire up the range, fry up some bacon and potatoes, eat supper, drowse in the warmth and get away from this shuttered wreck. Behind us, the corrugated metal at the back of the Dutch barn is already holed with rust. A spare wheel from the redundant horse cart has been hastily commandeered as a bit of fence to keep wandering sheep away from Aunt Mary's precious hay. At our feet are other cast-offs, a sealed paint tin and a strewn pile of beach gravel readied for long-abandoned building works but now overgrown with weeds. This scattered wreckage is the last proof; the repeating generations, children born in this house and raised, adult years committed and spent, even the lives of dead waked and gone, all the life that flowed here, has ceased. Sonny presses down on the silver button and takes the picture. We hear the click of the shutter and the wind of the film being pulled forward, impatient for this picture taking to be over. Michael, seven, is grim faced. Perhaps he has an intimation, despite the day's frantic labour, of what the adults cannot say even to themselves; everything is in vain and our future on the island is finished. We are standing in the picture of our ruin.

INTIMATIONS

I was Lucky once.

Death first came for me in a summer plague, and a small barking cough. I was eleven years old and from somewhere in the city air – a splutter, a wheeze – I contracted an ancient infection, *Mycobacterium tuberculosis*, and began to die.

Tuberculosis is a bacteria, a microorganism, that has afflicted humanity for aeons and killed millions of the poor, the malnourished and the susceptible. Tuberculosis infected Neolithic society and killed the Egyptian Pharaoh Akhenaten and his wife Nefertiti. The ancient Greeks knew the disease as *phthisis* – wasting. Tuberculosis remains one of the great diseases of humanity. One third of the world's population is latently infected with the rod-shaped *tubercle bacillus* in their lungs, but less than 10 per cent are likely to develop the disease.

Tuberculosis is a pathogen of a weakened immune system, an invader that bursts out from within the body's tissue when our defences are down. In the polluted cities of Victorian England, and across the industrialising world, tuberculosis killed one in four of the population. Tuberculosis' popular name in English was *consumption,* a shorthand for the sweating night fevers, ravaging weight loss and physical decay the bacteria malingeringly inflicts on its host. Tuberculosis incubates, slowly attacking the lungs and other organs, causing pus-filled necrotic lesions in delicate tissues, the coughing up of blood and, finally, death. As they gasp and spit their way to the grave, the diseased cough up fresh colonies of bacterium ready to infect others.

By the late nineteenth and early twentieth centuries, there was no cure. The standard treatment for tuberculosis was to confine and isolate the infectious away from the general population in special hospitals and sanatoriums until they recovered, or died. The first TB sanatorium opened in Poland in 1863 and the same medical isolation regime was soon copied around the world. The dying were being hidden away behind high walls and closed doors as part of the growing power of the Western Death Machine.

In 1943, twenty-three-year-old graduate student Albert Schatz, a soil microbiologist working at Rutgers University in New Jersey, isolated the *streptomycin* microbe, an antibiotic particularly lethal to *Mycobacterium tuberculosis.* The antibiotic, given in combination with two other drugs, was a medical revolution; an astounding miracle cure. The incurably sick, locked away in sanatoriums, got better and went home.

From the 1950s onwards, tuberculosis dwindled across the Western world, and by the 1970s it was so rare that my city doctors refused at first to believe that my small barking cough was anything other than a summer chest infection. My symptoms, the doctors conceded, were puzzling, but if I really had tuberculosis I would have been feverish, coughing up blood-streaked sputum and losing weight. I had none of these symptoms – just the cough. But on my mother's insistence – she worked as a nurse – I was duly X-rayed. When the result arrived – showing a suspicious tubercular shadow on my left lung – I was shipped that same afternoon to the city's dilapidated old sanatorium for further tests. I had fallen victim to a forgotten enemy, the White Death, and through my infection become a danger to the rest of humanity.

Formerly known as the City Fever Hospital, the sanatorium's heyday had been in the 1930s when it was crammed with the contagious. Surrounded by high walls and lavish grounds, a *cordon sanitaire* between its spluttering occupants and the outside world, the re-named City Hospital had been a world unto itself. The hospital was a sprawling complex of baronial stone, turreted buildings, isolation wings, pavilions and segregated wards housing hundreds of patients. There was a day centre, a ballroom, a pool hall and communal dining rooms to occupy the inmates' potential years of medical isolation. Hidden away somewhere in the lush jungle greenery was also a morgue. City Hospital was the ascendant Western Death Machine.

By the time I arrived, City Hospital was in trouble. Schatz's wonder drug had cured the sick, emptied the wards, fired half the staff and starved the hospital of funds. Three decades on, City was a shrinking, decaying hulk ready for the bulldozers. Cancer, not contagion, was now the mainstay, and the once teeming ward for tubercular children long since closed. In my potential infectiousness, I was still deemed too dangerous to go anywhere else. With no other option, I went straight on to the adult Male Chest ward to await further tests.

I was a unique minority of one, an eleven-year-old marooned within a livid charnel house of middle-aged mucus-heaving, lung-slashed, flesh-gouged, cancer-dying, spitting-gobbing bronchitics. Having become infected by the remnants of one waning global epidemic, I arrived into the epicentre of another. Lung cancer was reaching its global historical peak and my fellow patients were victims of the Western world's then near universal addiction to *Nicotiana tabacum*. One in four deaths, akin to tuberculosis in the previous century, could be attributed to tobacco-related cancer.

My new companions weren't on the ward to pass their hours in languid tubercular afternoon tea dances. After being puffed on, tarred over, irritated, singed by hot gases and poisoned by tobacco smoke for decades, the cells of their smoker's bodies had slipped the bounds of regulated mitosis and turned cancerous; lungs, lips, throat, oesophagus and jaw. They were

pilgrims shuffling along on a via dolorosa awaiting sur-
geries, further tests on more ominous shadows on their
lungs, remissions, relapses, confirmations of metastatic
cancer outbreaks in other organs, bouts of primitive
toxic chemotherapy and radiation blasts on their dwindling real estate – their bodies. To turn away from one
horror was to turn towards another. Like battle scars,
their first two forefingers were tarred brown from the
particular poisons of their choice; unfiltered Capstan
Full Strength, blue and white Embassy Regals, the
cheaper dark green Number 6 or the seemingly luxurious but no less toxic gold packages of Benson & Hedges
cigarettes.

This hellish antechamber, fifty beds jammed in,
lined up and facing each other on either side of a T-style
extension wing off the main hospital corridor, was fully
booked for the passage out. I was lucky to get a bed.

In daylight, death had no dominion over the ward's
iron discipline. Every hour ran to the same go-stop
ritual. At 7 a.m. the nurses called morning reveille
and forcibly roused the indolent ambulatory out of
bed. Bowels and bladders were emptied and bedpans
delivered and exchanged. Temperatures were taken
and morning pills prescribed. Breakfast was served
and cleared, and the ward returned to a determined
order by the white-uniformed nurses prior to our daily
medical visitation. As the breakfast dishes rolled away,

a tense expectancy, a gnawing anticipation, would begin ahead of the day's main ceremonial event – the Morning Ward Round. Sometime after nine, but never precise enough to be calculable, the white-coated consultant and his young doctor team would stroll onto the ward like a squad of inspectors. Perversely, every patient longed to be chosen by this fleeting medical caravan. We were grateful for the attention. News, even of our own terminal condition, was progress against the limitless emptiness. It was always a disappointment, a slight, to be passed over; even our terminal disease had failed to be of interest.

Every bedside consultation would begin with the inscrutable hieroglyphics from the bottom-of-the-bed temperature charts that logged our daily existence. With the case notes in his hand, one of the junior doctors would outline his diagnosis for his consultant as the team peered down on the patient. The doctors openly spoke a coded language of unintelligible medical terms; *micturition, adenocarcinoma metastatic invasion, stage four, squamous cell.* Parts of the body being examined would then be uncovered on request and portions prodded or felt for further malignancies. Wounds were scrutinised and the examination continued until the verdict agreed. Occasionally a patient was asked about possible symptoms, but usually only to confirm the predetermined verdict. Our role as patients, we understood, was to be acted upon. To be

passively and eternally grateful to the doctors for whatever was about to be inflicted in hope of redemption.
In return for our compliance, each examined patient
was allowed to ask two or three questions; particular
difficulties swallowing or the purported size of the
alien lump inside them, a prune or a peach, and the
likelihood of discharge home. Declarations of fears of
imminent morbidity were never voiced. We took our
orders in blank, often uncomprehending, silence. After
a suitable interval, the medical cortege moved on to
the next patient.

After the ward round came lunch, served up half cold
from stainless steel heat trolleys porter-pushed from
the distant kitchens; industrial mince, stewed carrots,
boiled potatoes, followed by tea and another bedpan
round. Every meal was served at your bedside. Supper
was another version of lunch; a tasteless slice of meat
swimming in brown glutinous gravy, over-stewed vegetables gone cold, sodden mash and a custard dessert.
Teams of auxiliary nurses came and went, clearing
dishes, mopping floors, freshening water jugs and
doling out tea and biscuits. Meanwhile their superiors,
qualified nurses with bosom-pinned watches, tight
green waistbands and starched white flaring apron
dresses, measured out the daily drug intake from the
Drugs Chest. Or they passed out thermometers and
took blood pressures in so many cycles of repetition
that the order of time crumbled.

Everything on Male Chest was faded, second hand, worn. The pale green walls, the light blue bed covers, the once bluish-grey Formica on top of the bedside lockers, had bleached out in the repeated tide of so many bodies. The wooden sides of anything were bashed and bruised, metal was scratched and fabrics thinned. The smell of disinfectant, bowels and over-boiled food lingered on in the overheated window-sealed air. Our few possessions were reduced to a toothbrush, toiletries and a borrowed book housed in the top drawer of our bedside lockers. In the lower drawer we archived the last tokens of our outside lives; the clothes we had worn on the day we arrived. Our daily uniforms, striped pyjamas of various hues, dressing gowns and leather slippers, had rotted away to an amorphous grey and, like us, lost all definition of former selves.

Our lives shrank to ten foot by eight foot of floor space, the boundaries of our bed curtains, abutted on either side by other patients. Presumably for reasons of morale, only the bedridden were allowed to lie down and sleep through the day. The walking wounded had to be on our feet or, more realistically, sitting up to attention in bedside chairs. Time dragged, the hours slowed, minutes grew and each day merged into the blank emptiness of the predecessor. Change was confined to the shifting rotas of day and night nurses, and a separate weekly trolley loaded with well-thumbed hardbacks from the hospital library. There were no bars on the window or locks on the doors, but it made no difference. Powerless, stilled, immobilised, even the walking wheezy were too weak to stagger far. Our world was circumscribed by the toilets at the top of the ward and the glassed-in television room in the bottom right corner that ran out the test card from two o'clock in the afternoon until the lights dimmed at ten. Child and adults we shared in the hollowness of vacant time. Male Chest was our living tomb.

At night on the open ward there was no disguising death's imminence.

Sshhhhragggg.

Sshhhraggg.

The noise would begin with a rasping, frothy *sshhhhragggg*, as the drowning owner sought to gather the overwhelming choking sputum into their throat from their lungs.

Sshhhhragggg . . .

Sshhhhragggg.

The same sound, the racking noise of congested lungs gasping against their drowned entombment would crescendo, again and again, as oesophagi were clenched and gargled with remaining breath to clear blocked windpipes.

Sshhhhragggg . . . sshhhhragggg . . . shhhhragggg . . . sshhhhragggg.

After the *sshhhhragggg* there would be a moment's

71

silence and then a *grrrrhhhhh,* finished off with a sibilant *thupp* spit into the standard-issue paper cup spittoon. The cymbals of a breath-squeezed wheezing *Ahoo . . . ahoo . . . ahoo . . . ahoo, ahi . . . ahoo . . . ahi . . . caw . . . huh . . . huh . . . ahoo,* followed by a stutter-gun of explosive hacking from deep in surgically sheared lungs, would break out in another section of the mortal orchestra. One dying patient after another would awaken until the walls filled up with a machine-gun guttural cacophony of horror.

In the gloom of the ward night lights, I would lie in bed with my hands over my ears and try hard not to listen.

I was a boy awaiting puberty. The bodies I had seen on the island at wakes were old men and women who were strangers; aged adults whose death, in my child's thinking, was part of some unexplained but natural process. On Male Chest I felt caged up in the same cell as a terrifying wild animal. I was afraid of becoming another one of those choking, suffocating lungs in the night. I wanted to escape this place. So I distanced myself with a mental *cordon sanitaire.* I stared straight ahead, head up, as I marched through the ward, avoiding looking at things; the small bald-headed man, Albert, in the middle of the ward on the right-hand side, whose dressing gown fell away to reveal what I first thought were little bald baby legs before recognising them as bandaged stumps cut high on his thighs. I glanced away from the oozing red scars on bellies and backs, where some cancerous tentacle had been cut out of pasty-white middle-aged flesh. I studiously looked away from Derek, my neighbour, a former postman with half a lung, as he pursed slack blubbery lips and spat into his waxed paper spittoon cup. The spittoons were for collecting our mucus to be tested to help identify the exact squamous cell or bacteria at work in shortening our lives. Spitting into them was another of the ward's orders, but I had a recurrent nightmare that in the night I would mistake Derek's spittoon for my water glass.

Comings and goings, the death and passage of a fellow patient, was announced by the pulling of curtains a day or two before their demise, sealing them off from our sight. Relatives, marked out as civilians by their street clothes, would appear at odd hours and then disappear behind the green veil. Not long after this sheathing, auxiliaries would casually pass on, over the changing of bed pans and doling out of dinner, the obvious news that:

'Frank, in bed forty-three, is a bit poorly.'

The life of the ward would carry on undisturbed around this fabric blockade. Unfamiliar porters would finally arrive with the 'death wagon' – a solid-sided trolley that hid the corpse in a special cavity – delve behind the curtain and withdraw fully loaded. Curtains would be pulled, the bed relaundered, locker cleared, and, after a decent interval, a morning or an afternoon, a new resident would be seamlessly installed.

Tuberculosis is a slow killer and its bacteria take a long time to divide and grow. In between not looking and not hearing, I had more tests, more X-rays, and spat on command into the spittoon in hope of providing a testable sample of my disease. The doctors did a pleural tap – using a long needle to draw infected fluid from the bottom of my lungs – then sent the result off. The bacilli from my lungs had to be cultured, grown for two months in a petri dish like a little plant colony and then tested. If the result proved positive, my diagnosis would be known and I could potentially be cured. No one mentioned the other possibility.

I hung on along with the disease incubating inside my body, waiting for each long-lighted summer day to pass into another. Unlike my fellow patients, I was able to escape the ward as long I never left the hospital grounds. I would change into my outside clothes and go on expeditions to explore the sprawling wreck of the hospital's past. Wings had been amputated, wards lopped off and pavilions abandoned. Trees, creeper vines and rhododendron bushes jungle-like were already reclaiming every institutional cast-off.

I hacked my way through the foliage and broke into the disused former day centre, the noticeboards advertising afternoon tea dances for long-departed patients. I played snooker against myself for hours in a damp recreation room on a baize-ripped table. I found a loosened side door into the former female TB ward and explored the ruins; a communal bathroom where a desiccated pink soap lay in a shower soap holder and a forgotten blue dressing gown hung from the back of the stall. Old iron beds were piled up and gathering dust, leaks in the roof had rotted the floor and mouldy patient folders filled with indecipherable blue biro notes were scattered across the lost command of the central nurses' station. Everything in these ghost wards was a record of a redundant past. Except for me.

I had been left behind, still infected. My expeditions were always circular; I ended up back at my chair and bed staring at the clock at the top of the ward whose hands had barely moved.

Somewhere in that open-ended time, one of the dying men adopted me as a mascot, a worthy cause. Jimmy 'Fingers' wheezed and shook as he chit-chatted about school, why I was on the ward and what I was planning to be in the life to come, before returning for bouts at his oxygen mask. I had never wanted to be a train driver, an astronaut or any of the typical ambitions of boyhood. On the ward those non-ambitions shrunk even further. I was lonely and just wanted to go home, though I had no idea how that could happen. Even talking about a life outside the ward, a world to return to, was an inconceivable act of hope. To cheer me up and maybe to feed me up, Jimmy passed on his regular bounty of perfectly vivid Snow-White-red apples and bowls of exotic green grapes bought for him by his visitors. The apples were hard on his dentures anyway, but the kindness was real. Jimmy had very few powers left and little else to give; tied to the oxygen mask, he could never stray far or too long from his bed. In return I made myself useful to Jimmy and other patients by running errands to the distant hospital shop for their daily newspapers and cigarettes.

Jimmy, a dapper character who had worked in a bookies, tipped well and kept up appearances by combing his hair, dabbing on Old Spice aftershave and croakily flirting with the nurses. Jimmy looked old to me, but was probably only in his late forties. He lived on the left-hand side of the ward opposite Albert, the stumpy-legged man, so talking to Jimmy with my back to the right was a good way of never catching sight of cut-off legs. Jimmy was about five foot nine with broad shoulders and said he 'loved the ladies'. He insisted on wearing his own pyjamas rather than the industrially battered garments handed over weekly at the laundry hatch. Over the top he wore a red tartan dressing gown taken from home. Jimmy was soon my best customer. Daily I would take his order – the paper, a packet of mints, a bottle of juice, a pack of cigarettes and 'some sweeties for yourself'. I would tramp off, eager to have something to do to break the monotony of Male Chest, more than anything else.

After supper we all prepared for the magical ritual of the day: Visiting Hours, between seven and nine. We preened ourselves, tightening pyjama cords, combing hair, the older patients brushing dentures or tobacco-stained teeth. As anxious hosts we tidied our bed space, rearranged the wax spittoon behind the flower vase or sat up straighter ready for inspection. Would anyone come? Or would we be another of those sad losers dotted round the ward? Lying on their backs in beds, already half dead, calling out only for another bedpan; abandoned wrecks.

At seven, the ward doors opened and a stream of visitors entered in search of a brother, husband, father or son. Once he was found, these strange travellers clustered, borrowed chairs, plumped up pillows, passed over gifts of fruit or sweets and ran back and forth to the tea trolley. Huddled within the attention of these fabulous ambassadors, each patient was *someone* again. Each bed space became a world entire unto itself. Whatever passed between patient and visitors, private and precious. For fear of cross infection, my siblings had been banned by the doctors; my pool of visitors restricted to my mother. My longing to see her was intense. On the nights she failed to appear I burst into uncontrollable weeping and had to be comforted by the nurses.

Jimmy was fastidious in his preparations for the evening entertainment. He dabbed on Brylcreem and brushed down his dressing gown. I am sure he would have ironed his pyjamas if he could. His regular visitors, a glamorous blonde woman and an older woman, maybe her mother, fussed over him, kissed and squeezed him, as if they were on a date. Jimmy would almost have looked flash if the tartan gown were not now several sizes too big for him. It hung off his shoulders, its looseness accentuating the scrawniness of the neck that rose from within its folds. There was an ugly scar on his neck and his voice was dry and hoarse, his vocal cords like bits of sandpaper rubbing together. But Jimmy held himself defiant, holding court, laughing until he exploded in terrifying, lung-breaking coughs.

Time, for once, passed in a blur until our visitors, huddle by huddle, began to leave, and the waning light outside and the arm of the ward clock signalled the visit over. Five minutes before nine an auxiliary would walk the ward warning the remaining visitors that their time was running out. There would be awkward hugs and kisses. Last-minute stragglers, usually Jimmy's, called out promises of return as they made for the exit amidst the departing clack of stilettos, until the distant sound of the far ward door died away into leaden silence.

At some moment malignant sadness would descend as the crushing dominion of Male Chest reasserted sovereignty over us. We were back in our washed out purgatory. Trapped. Then, as if to distract its prisoners, the machine of the ward would spring into action; the clatter of the night drugs chest, the dispensing of bed-pans, temperatures and final tea rounds. Another night of fitful coughing lay ahead. And the aloneness of those hours we would each, men and child, endure.

In the daytime, rituals were invented to fill the empty hours. Patients doggedly left their beds to gather in the glassed-in television-cum-smoking room for another cigarette. The past is another country we can never visit but, even at this distance, it is incredible to believe that a lung cancer ward would have its own designated smoking lounge. The day lounge too was tattered and worn, the varnish on the wooden arms of the not-very-leather red chairs burned and singed by trails of the forgotten perched cigarettes of long-dead smokers. High on the wall, a silent TV relentlessly beamed the test card through the slow hours of the afternoon.

Jimmy's trips to the smoking room were always marked with nonchalant grace. He would dispense with his oxygen mask and slowly stroll over as if on his way to a good night out. Unlike the others who plumped down exhausted in the seats, Jimmy always liked to smoke standing up. He would begin with the careful assembly of the hit. A flattened cigarette packet or one limp, fraying cigarette would be pulled from the pocket of that snazzy tartan dressing gown. Delving on the other side, he'd retrieve the last real remnant of his lost life – his oblong gold lighter.

Jimmy's hands would move together and his head lower in perfect synchronicity like a scene from a Humphrey Bogart movie. The lighter would strike. A burst of flame. Jimmy would suck on the cigarette tip and the end would flare red. This was Jimmy's favourite moment; a point of happiness, a re-enactment of his old life beyond these confines. Then, as the smoke hit the last bit of functioning lung, he'd burst out in splutters, choking wheezing coughs, a rasping rat-ta-tat-tat of suffocation. His face would switch colour from white to puce as if a madman's hands were on his neck. His eyes would contort; his arms involuntarily flail, quickly followed by a series of heaving agonies, explosive exhalations and desperate sharp intakes of breath. The attack would last for ninety seconds and then Jimmy would settle down, calm, and try another puff.

These dying smokes must have exacerbated my fellow patients' already breathless grasp on life, but most of them were too far gone to care. Their suicidal smoking was an act of remembrance and acceptance. A moment of jocular grace on the cellular scaffold. Any self-deceit, or talk of hope, had expired. There was no road to recovery, just whatever lay ahead. Jimmy, with or without his oxygen mask, and his fellow smokers would all die here in the embrace of the Western Death

Machine. They were never going home. These last cigarettes were a defiant prayer to themselves and their
lives gone by.

After two months on the ward my results came back.
I was declared to have tuberculosis; safely diagnosed
with a dangerous but curable disease. I owe my life to
Albert Schatz's discovery. I was to be discharged the
following day. That night in the television room I told
Jimmy I would be gone in the morning. He was un-
characteristically sitting down, not smoking, and he
had just finished combing his hair.

'That's good son. I knew you'd make it out of here.
You wouldn't want to be ending up like this lot of losers.
Don't waste it, son.'

And then he smiled.

In the morning, as I was passing through the ward to
leave, I looked out for Jimmy to say goodbye and thank
him. He wasn't at his bed. Maybe he was off for another
X-ray or a private chat with his doctors. Instead there
was his empty bed and yesterday's paper. I walked
out, passed through the final *cordon sanitaire* of leafy
grounds out into the street, holding my mother's hand.
We waited at the bus stop and caught a city bus back to
my life as a child. I never saw Jimmy or any of the other
Male Chest patients again.

Everyone I met on my long summer of plague on
Male Chest is dead; Jimmy, the other patients, the

white-coated doctors and nurses. Cancer or decades of time have overtaken them. Schatz's wonder drug is no longer a miracle cure. New drug-resistant variants of *Mycobacterium tuberculosis* again pose a threat to new generations of the poor, the malnourished and the susceptible. City Hospital, like its sister sanatoriums around the world, is long gone, its buildings demolished or converted into fancy apartments. Nothing remains but old archives and a memory of how death on Male Chest was all around me, so close you only had to reach out and touch it, the barely living and the dying jammed in, powerless, imprisoned together. By chance, and with the grace and help of an adoptive father, I was the only one to escape. A boy on a death ward who could not see his small, barking, summer cough as his end, and like an innocent child in a fairy story passed unscathed through a dark wood full of monsters.

I was very Lucky once.

EXILES

Every summer we came lumbering home to the island as a tribe. Sonny would borrow his firm's twelve-seater diesel van and pack the inward-facing hard wooden seats with as much human cargo as the vehicle could hold. We were rarely fewer than ten squabbling children – second cousins, foster sisters and brothers, enmeshed somewhere in a clan web – alternately, and sometimes simultaneously, throwing up or pleading for the windows to be lowered to prevent the effusion of more vomit; demanding sick bags, instant toilet breaks or the exact distance to our destination. All crushed between the hefty bodies of our aunties, Aunt Maggie and Aunt Brigid. Or the three Lavelle sisters, Maud, Mary and Bridget, who had worked in the same chocolate factory as my mother and whose conversations always steered, in lowered voices, towards gynaecological conditions. Bridget's husband had left her, but because of her religion, our religion, Bridget could never get a divorce. The plainer Maud and Mary had never married. Spinsters. Maiden aunts who all their lives shared the same table, sofa, room, toilet and bed. The Three Sisters, as we called them, had over the years, like the

Fates, become so telepathically attuned to the cadences of each other that each was perfectly able to follow on from the words of her flagging sister, thus leaving no gaps, pauses or hesitation. We became their substitute children, to be indulged on the long journey home with winks and hard-boiled sweets slyly passed in defiance of my mother's prohibitions.

In later years, the same web of clan and familial obligation would demand a statutory visit for downy-cheeked old ladies' kisses with my Lavelle 'aunties' when they, too, had come home to live and quietly die, one by one, on the island. The sisters were fond of me, a child turned teenager whom they had known since birth, a never-son-that-could-have-been. Embarrassingly, almost coquettishly, in gratitude of my visits, they would lavish praise on my looks to each other – my height, my examination results and my potential prospects with girls.

'Will ya look at the curls on him.'

'What I'd give to have that head of hair.'

'Mary, stop, you're making him blush.'

Tea would be drawn and neat plates of biscuits and cake urged upon me at their cramped dining table as we spoke of their days, our journeys across the Irish Sea together and my life back in the city far, far away. Maybe they were lonely for the life they had left behind, or just excited to have a visitor to pass the time. Looking back, the bonds between us – three Irish spinsters and a teenage boy – reached beyond blood and across the generations because we were all part of something greater than each of us, the web of belonging of Home.

In the city we lived in a second-floor sprawling tenement apartment, my parent's lives circumscribed by their jobs and the demands of their seven children. The city gave us all the opportunities, schools and universities, that the island never could. But it never won our hearts.

Home, the island, was not a holiday destination. It was a fabulous zoo filled with clucking hens and their freshly laid, warm eggs. There were grunting pigs being fed household scraps and cows who lifted their tails and pissed out a river of steaming urine into the trough of my maternal grandfather Pat Martin's stable. There were fields to roam, lands that had been owned for generations, cows to be milked and sheep to be driven to pasture. Majestically, like a land-bound admiral, Pat Martin would scan Slievemore mountain with his extending brass telescope, which hung on the back of the door in Ballinasally, in search of Dolly, his fence-bounding horse. My maternal grandmother, Tilly, a short, stout woman who dressed in a shawl, scarf and hessian apron and looked the full part of what she was – an Irish peasant – cooked over an open fire, hefting pots of green potatoes for her chickens and blackened kettles for tea onto soot-encrusted bars over the flames.

The taste of everything – unpasteurised milk, butter, searing yellow egg yolks – was different. Strange vans, smelling of fruit cake, ripe bananas and marzipan, called at the door. The driver would beep the horn and you would rush to the road stepping into this marvellous shelved travelling emporium so Tilly, like other villagers, could stock up on fat bacon rashers, sausages, tea, sugar or artillery-shaped bottles of apple-flavoured Cidona. And be softly blackmailed by her grandchild into buying sweets.

At my Aunt Mary's in Cabaun we slept three to bed, the sheer number of summer visitors – exiled offspring, nieces, nephews, cousins – overwhelming the house. We ate serial meals of boiled potatoes and over-roasted meat seated at long wooden benches in the back kitchen as Glen and Major, two sheepdogs, and a squad of cats snapped at our feet begging for bones.

We provoked the wrath of my other grandfather, Pat Toolis, as he reigned in old age from a wooden chair next to the turf range, squabbling over card games of Twenty-Five, playing for match heads until the long western light died in the ocean. And it was time for bed. Often we were taken visiting to a roster of other relatives; Uncle Edward, who was born in Manhattan but in defiance of the flow had re-emigrated to Ireland; or Liam, a long-term bachelor, whose cow stable shared the end of his narrow house – the heat of his four cows reaching through the wall to warm him during the winter. We went to hillside shrines and bottled Holy Water from sacred wells.

I was taken to my first wake, my first sight of the dead, when I was seven by my mother. The wake house was a small white-washed farmhouse in the village of Ballinasally, where my mother was born. Inside, the rooms were packed; old men in flat caps and scuffed jackets, old women with whiskers and vivid red or green scarves knotted under their chin, sitting in a line of wooden chairs. I hung close to my mother, bewildered by the hand shaking, the soft cries of mourning, the tears and the chorus of black-shrouded women we passed in turn. The open coffin was laid out in the sitting room on the broad planks of the kitchen table. I watched my mother bless herself at the head of the coffin and pray. She reached down with her lips and kissed whatever was inside. I wasn't tall for my age and couldn't see over the side of the coffin. She urged me to follow her. As I came forward she whispered.

'Bless yourself. And make a sign of the Cross.'

I had to go up on tiptoes to reach over the edge of the coffin. Inside, there was an old man with dry skin. His face was a strange colour, unnatural. He lay perfectly immobile, dressed in a suit, but I knew he was not asleep. He was too still, a statue. Lower down on his chest a string of grey shiny rosary beads were wrapped between long, pointed, bloodless fingers. The knotted fingers and nails on his right hand were browned with the same stain of tobacco that marked the island's heavy smokers. I was instinctively afraid and held back.

'You should touch him.'

As if to show I would come to no harm, my mother put her hand out and stroked the corpse's face.

'Kiss him. It will take away the fear.'

Straining on my toes, I reached in and put my lips against the flat of his forehead for a moment. The coldness of his skin stung and I startled back.

My mother had her hand on my shoulder.

'Now just say a prayer for the poor man's soul,' she said.

I closed my eyes, made the sign of the Cross, and mumbled my way through a Hail Mary. As I opened my eyes and looked around, I saw two old ladies smiling back at me. In the mixture of superstition, pagan and Catholic belief, many islanders believed the prayers of children, the sexually innocent, had a greater power to rise to heaven for the benefit of the deceased's soul. The old ladies called out to my mother and made space for her to sit down beside them. Plates of cigarettes, spilled out in a circular pattern, were passed from hand to hand along with bowls of snuff. Tea and sandwiches came amidst talk of who had emigrated and what had happened to them. How the woman, a childhood friend, was now married and living away somewhere in England and how many children she had.

I grew bored and stood on the floor between my

mother's knees watching the other mourners arrive; an old man, with a cane, taking off his flat cap and praying at the head of the coffin. The gleaming white baldness of his head now further marked by the mid-forehead scar of the line of his cap on his sun-weathered face. The wake was going on all around us, a stream of mourners arriving and leaving. My mother's death-teaching was already over, swallowed up in the domestic chatter of shared lives on an island where the sight of the dead, in their very ordinariness, was as natural as the rain showers of summer.

As a child, I longed to escape going 'visiting'; obligatory rounds of old ladies to kiss and tea and biscuits to be drunk in strange houses, whether at a wake or family gathering. I couldn't see these substitute 'uncles' and 'aunties' for who they were; a people bound in community that, despite the bleeding out into exile, reassembled itself whenever and wherever it could. The 'living away' in foreign lands was part of every islander's life. But the belonging of Home, the map of the generations, the bonds of blood and time, reached out beyond the island to embrace the community's children, and their children too, wherever they were in the world. The dead, their wakes and funerals, were all part of the same bonding. The unravelling had its casualties; many islanders never returned and their children fell away like autumn leaves off a tree. But if you wanted to, you could reach out and pull yourself in. Home was never far away.

The connection could work both ways. Smoking away in the back corner of the island-bound van on the journey homewards was another familiar Irish character: the Lodger, Mary Johnson, from the remote village of Dooega on the far side of the Minaun. Mary Johnson, we never called her just by her first name, had arrived at the family doorstep one morning long before in search of a bed. A stranger alone in a strange city, whose only asset was an address bearing some connection to her native island. The address was my mother's, and through communal obligation Mary Johnson made it over the threshold. The overnight bed became a room and Mary Johnson a permanent lodger who lived for a decade or more, as resented interloper and unwanted guest, amidst the chaos of our crowded family tenement flat. And to whose room – off-limits to my parents – my teenage sisters would retire for a sly smoke.

The journey home took us through the other Ireland we called 'the North' where the Troubles raged and tribal badlands were marked out in Protestant red, white and blue painted kerbstones. Marauding British Army patrols armed for combat would appear out of border hedgerows and politely ask for Sonny's licence. These glimpses of war beyond the windscreen, even the Irish tricolour-daubed Catholic enclaves, always

made the adults nervous. Everyone breathed an exag-
gerated sigh of relief when we reached the border at
the abandoned, long IRA-bombed British customs post
at Belcoo in Fermanagh. We crossed a small stream,
and after another fifty yards turned sharp right at the
sleepy gardai post in Blacklion. We had entered another
country, the South. The 'real Ireland', as we called it.

After a few hundred yards of tarred pretence, the
road collapsed into a 150-mile long string of pothole
held together by crumbling tarmac. Cows and men on
bicycles became masters of the thoroughfare. Unkempt
vegetation burst out from unkempt hedgerows. Sonny
laboured to negotiate perpetual makeshift roadworks
with their juddering ramps, gravel chips and barriers of
oil drums. We squeezed our way through the choked
main streets of middle Ireland, past shops festooned
with bright yellow gas bottles, turf briquettes and rotting vegetables. We counted off the names by heart
– Manorhamilton, Sligo, Ballysadare, Charlestown,
Swinford, Bohola, Castlebar, Newport – as Sonny
warily tried not to lose his way in the wilderness of un-
signposted roads. To soften the journey, Sonny would
reel off one romantic ballad after another, urging us
all to sing along. The black steering wheel would slip
through his weathered workman hands and his voice,
strong, sonorous, clear, would rise above the drone of
the diesel engine, conjuring hillsides, maidens and the
frailty of young love.

*

Will you go lassie go,
And we'll all go together to pluck wild mountain thyme
All around the blooming heather
Will you go lassie go
And we'll all go together to gather wild mountain thyme
All around the blooming heather.

Reluctantly at first, but then, with his encouragement, we would all join in and the lumbering van filled with the sound of childish voices. In the green patches of countryside between towns we would look out for the painted white and blue roadside shrines to the Virgin Mary, her eyes and fleshy concrete hands lifted towards heaven. Often, just inches from the road, we would see people on their knees reciting the early evening rosary. Praying openly to God and Our Lady.

This Ireland really was another country.

Our last stop before the island was always the little town of Newport. My mother would buy mounds of meat, thick rashers and fat sausages from Kelly's, the local butcher, who stayed open until ten at night lest famished townsfolk ran out of meat after evening Mass or fancied a fry-up just before hitting the bars. And it was in Newport that we always picked up the first real scent of home – the drift of peat smoke on the wind. Exhausted by the fourteen-hour journey, we children would quieten and finally fall asleep across the near-est auntie's lap, as Sonny at the wheel would plunge on into the west. Until the continent of Europe ran into the great ocean back the shore at Dookinella and our ears filled with the roar of the surf and above our heads the great reef of stars of the Milky Way lit the heavens.

RUINS

The house in Dookinella was close to falling down when my grandfather decided, with Uncle John gone, to pass the ruin on to Sonny, his first-born son. Built in 1937 from harvested beachstone, cement, lime, plaster and tile, the house was a simple three-room design; an oblong box with a basic sitting room/kitchen in the centre and a bedroom either side. A flat-roofed kitchen extension had been added in the 1950s. The years of cold abandonment and onslaught of winter storms had already begun to destroy the house from within. The porch and the back-kitchen extensions were falling down and the ceiling timbers eaten away by termites. Wood lice, beetles and assorted creepy-crawlies ascended and descended in torrents from ceiling to floor. Damp penetrated the floors and walls, mould grew like a fur coat on window sills, the chimneys needed rebuilding, the roof leaked and there was no inside water, bathroom or toilet. Undeterred, Sonny seized his life's chance to rebuild his childhood home.

With seven children, he never had much spare cash, but he was a gatherer, a careful hoarder who foraged the building sites he worked on, picking up a roll of cable here or a set of reinforcing rods there. Sonny was frugal; nothing of potential purpose was thrown away but carefully set aside in readiness for the next run to the island. To ferry his materials across the Irish Sea he was always building cumbersome roof racks or car-sized trailers to attach to the firm's borrowed van. And then every summer Sonny would arrive with his treasure hoard of materials intent on tackling one or all of Dookinella's many failings.

On holiday he was always working; laying floors, plumbing in a toilet, lowering ceilings, shifting doorways, and frequently changing his mind as to the exact position of everything. The imperial fittings he had taken from the city would not match the missing metric parts on sale on the island's hardware store. Parts and adapters would have to be ordered, and despite the salesman's promises would never appear before the end of our summer.

I was his reluctant teenage apprentice. Sonny would ask me to help hold something down, a piece of wood or a length of metal, as he sawed and screwed at the other end. I'd acquiesce but would soon grow bored.

'My arm's sore. How long is this going to go on?' I would whine.

I'd be awkward or, more accurately, *contrary*, a word islanders used to describe argumentative drunks or tantrum-prone teenage children. Sonny would grow exasperated and release me from my task. My selfishness must have cut him; he was working to save the old house for all of his family, but Sonny never shouted or denounced me for my failures. He would just turn away and get on with the work himself.

Our summer visits were always too short to complete the bigger jobs. Sonny would parcel out the remainder of the work to Uncle Eddie or another relative, but it would never get done. Despite the clearest of instructions, the new floor levels would be wrong or the workmen would fail to leave the vital channel for the central heating pipe. Or the salt air would have corroded and seized the now useless but otherwise pristine oil boiler. The winter rain would again leach through a newly replastered wall. And so next summer the frenetic concrete-bashing would begin all over again. Sonny never gave up and slowly, ever so slowly, the spiralling decay of Dookinella was overtaken by his unending labours.

Our leave-taking came with its own bitter rituals. We would pack and close up Dookinella early, and Sonny would drive from house to house through the neighbouring villages of River and Cabaun, picking up the Lavelle sisters and any other stray city children who had come over on the boat with us. The last stop was always my maternal grandfather's house in Ballinasally. After the loading of the last suitcases in the trailer, Tilly would come out onto the road and stand beside the van weeping. My mother and my Aunt Brigid would follow in floods of tears. The wrench of this parting felt like betrayal. Grandfather Toolis at least had my Aunt Mary to look after him, but Tilly and Pat Martin were on their own. Alone together in their old age, growing older and frailer, their daughters scattered, living distant city lives. There was no one left to inherit their small farm; this house would die with them. Their weeping was a price of our exile. With the long journey ahead, and a ferry to catch, Sonny would gun the engine and slowly drive away, all of us waving through the back windows until the road dipped and we could no longer see the lone figure behind us. The mood of sorrow, amidst my mother and aunt's tears, wouldn't lift until we crossed onto the mainland and the island slipped away.

In our own Dookinella house, before we left, my mother had lit a turf fire in the hearth that would burn out untended and unseen behind us. This last fire was her parting gift to the house, a further few hours of flame and heat to keep the deep chill out, before its abandonment to the coming winter fury. This parting fire was a prayer, too, that the house would survive without us and we would return safe next year.

Below the house that Sonny rescued, closer to the ocean, just beyond the fields where I gathered hay as a child, lies the old village of Dookinella and a maze of drystone thatched houses dating from the 1700s. In the 1830s, the village, housing one of the few Catholic chapels on the whole island, had been a thriving community of more than 300 people, filling scores of houses.

Everything has fallen into ruin; the front and back walls of the houses are strewn rubble. All that remains, like identical rows of twin tombstones, are the old houses' gable ends; jutting up from the earth, marking out communal nettle and rock graves, enclosing emptiness, loss and departure. Every born soul is long scattered into the wind across the earth. Forever exiled, broken; their community, history, the island, lost to them. For some islanders, their new-found lives in America or England would be a gateway to a prosperity they could only have ever dreamed of. For others, many others, the perpetual instability of being a stranger in a strange land, the physical and mental punishment of being a despised Irish navvy or maid, the prejudice they would encounter and the perils of loneliness and alcoholism would destroy them. The toll of lives broken, shortened and lost would be measured out, decade after decade, in homeless hostels and hospital wards.

In saving an old house from collapse, Sonny saved something more precious than a roof and four walls. He saved a dream; the perpetual longing of all exiles, both past and future, for his children and their children to come – a road of return. That no matter where you lived, in what city or on what continent, or what catastrophe overtook you, there is a place, a land, a people, a refuge, a fire burning in a hearth, to come back to. Home.

CATASTROPHES

Death came for me again on the concrete stair of a hospital at 9 a.m. on a bright winter's morning, when I was nineteen.

Light was streaming in through a window and I was laughing at some joke with my younger sister Teresa. When we reached the hospital ward, the first thing I saw was my sister-in-law Marie silently waving her arms in the air. There was this grimace across her face. A nurse walked over and grabbed her arms as if, without that grasp, Marie would fly around the ward like a panicked bird, battering herself against the windows. Then this yelp came out of Marie's mouth:

'Bernard is dead!'

Bernard was my older brother, now lying in a side room a few feet away from where we stood. Marie and the nurse ran off the ward into an office – the matron's cosy parlour – and Teresa burst out crying. I just looked. Looked at the panic across the face of the nurses, the floorsweeping eyes of the housemen as they cowered in the staff room in order to avoid me. I saw their fear of death. I saw their fear of me as one of those associated with death and therefore mad and unpredictable.

101

I felt their intense desire to shoo us – me, my sister, my sister-in-law – into some box so that this awful chaos, this failure, this rupture, would not disturb the smooth running of the ward. And like a blade to the gut I knew then what the child on Male Chest had escaped. Death was alive in me.

When I was eighteen and still immortal, Bernard developed leukaemia. Leukaemia is a cancer, a mutation, of your white blood cells, which are produced by the body's bone marrow to help fight infections. Inside your bloodstream, cancerous cells called blasts multiply uncontrollably, supplanting healthy white blood cells until your immune system shuts down. An army of white cellular traitors fills every vein in your body. Leukaemia patients suffer from shortness of breath, repeated infections, extreme fatigue, anaemia, a low red blood cell count and a failure of their blood to clot. Their bodies bruise easily and any kind of wound is potentially life-threatening. They die of pneumonia or a haemorrhage in the brain or bleed out from every orifice. Leukaemia is not an easy death.

Bernard was amongst the first wave of patients in the world to receive a potentially life-saving bone marrow transplant. The procedure works by irradiating the patient's whole body, using one of those big X-ray cylinder machines, to kill off all the cancerous cells in their bone marrow. The cancerous marrow is then replaced with healthy marrow from a donor that closely matches the tissue type of the recipient. In theory, the donor marrow produces healthy white blood cells and the patient is cured.

I was my brother's donor; I was to save him with the marrow the doctors pumped out of my sternum and hips, under a general anaesthetic, in another cancer hospital filled with radiation-tanned young bald men who neither had hope of a transplant nor a life to come.

Other people die, not us. The world has order, a predictability. We live in the indefinite future-to-be; supper tonight, work tomorrow, your holidays booked for next year, mortgages paid and schools for the children. A life movie forever running ahead, in which we are automatically cast. Perhaps it's instinctive.

The other reel – that Azrael, the angel of death, is outside your front door at this moment, getting ready to break in with an axe and destroy your life – gets a lot less air-time. Bernard's illness, I thought, would be a heroic story of jeopardy, recovery and eventual triumph. I was almost callously indifferent towards him. I saw the complex medical preparations prior to his transplant as akin to an older brother's university tribulations; a bureaucratic roll-call of difficulties he would inevitably overcome. His potential dying was an intrusion on my life. I had no doubt, like in the movies, the engine would finally cough into life, the plane take off and the bullets miss. Or, at the last moment, a man in a white coat would run up the ward with the wonder drug, my bone marrow, and save the patient. My brother. And everyone would live happily ever after.

Except it did not turn out that way. Bernard became a far more common tale; an ordinary catastrophe of mortality amongst ordinary lives. Not a saw-it-on-the-news story. Nor a did-you-see-that-car-wreck-on-the-other-side-of-the-carriageway story. But a one-of-us,the-truck-coming-straight-at-you,the-wreckage-spiralling-into-the-air,hitting-everyone-in-the-face-and-body, gouging-wounds-that-never-healed sort of story.

It was summer when Bernard first went to his local doctor's surgery worried about his growing breathlessness – a hidden symptom of the cancer cells in his bloodstream crowding out the healthy red blood cells needed to carry oxygen. Inside the surgery, unknowingly waiting in the consultation room, was our eldest brother Francis, who was working extra hours as a GP locum on top of his hospital day job. Maybe Bernard knew his own brother would be on duty that night. Maybe he didn't. Bernard described his symptoms. In the physical exam, Francis could feel that Bernard had an enlarged spleen, a key indicator that Bernard was profoundly ill. But nothing was said. Both brothers, still in their twenties, read from a script that downplayed the seriousness of the moment. Francis sent Bernard off to hospital for blood tests. Two days later,

it was Francis in his day job as a hospital haematolo-
gist, specialising in the treatment of leukaemics, who
got the blood samples back. He fed them into the machines to measure Bernard's white blood cell count.
The first sample broke the scale; Bernard's bloodstream was so full of cancerous white blood cells that
technicians had to dilute the sample in half to bring
it back within measurable range. Bernard's diagnosis
was indisputable. He had chronic myeloid leukaemia
and without a transplant was going to die. Bernard was
twenty-six.

Bernard was lucky. He got more attention from other
medical staff and was selected for one of the precious
places on the bone marrow transplant programme.
Having a doctor brother who specialised in the disease
that was killing you helped. But Bernard's luck only
ran so far. Opting for a transplant had huge risks. It
was still a highly experimental treatment. Many transplant patients died within months of their operation.
The survival rate after five years was low. Bernard was
trading the certainty of three years of conventional
treatment before his certain death for the uncertainty
of a transplant; and hope. He was gambling his life now
for the possibility of a future. He never hesitated – he
chose the transplant.

The total body radiation killed Bernard's leukaemia
and the transplant sort of worked, but his compromised

immune system, which had to be suppressed with powerful drugs to avoid attacking my alien marrow, left him vulnerable to common infections. The gruelling treatment regimen was physically wearing – diarrhoea, weight loss, hair loss, constant nausea, twenty different tablets to be taken, the herpes, the rashes, the splutters and coughs, month after month, spiralled on and on till he shrunk down to a seven-stone walking skeleton. His luck ran out.

Bernard began to fear hospitals and the ever-rotating parade of doctors for whom he was not just a patient but also a fascinating experiment. When Bernard got another lung infection that February, seven months after his transplant, he didn't want to go back to hospital because he suspected he would die there. He was forced when the symptoms of what turned out to be a viral lung infection – shortness of breath – meant he had no choice. A big fan of crosswords, he wrote a kind of code to himself, a secret promise, based on the page numbers and entries in his favourite dictionary. The code was a string of numbers 598:22, 1494:8, 1302:10. The numbers on the left referred to the location of a specific word on the page. The number on the right was the page. After, I looked it up: I WILL SURVIVE.

Although I never understood why at the time, a few days after being admitted, Bernard was moved off the general ward into a private room. The cubicle was a dying space; a closable door, washed-out pink walls, a chipped bed frame, a bland bedside locker – an echo of the bleaching out of Male Chest – and white blankets; an institutional screen behind which death could be whispered. Bernard had been moved out of sight of the living. It was an act of kindness, and of denial; the grim open general medical ward beyond was engulfed in a geriatric winter flu epidemic. Bernard, by now an expert in hospital procedures, knew he would die there.

Bernard's final days were an agony without purpose, drowning in the viral fluid coating his lungs; every breath a gasp at the surface before being sucked under by the next wave. Like an AIDS patient, his compromised immune system could not resist this final viral attack.

Walking into the cubicle where Bernard lay as warm as you or I, just moments after the matron had seized my sister-in-law's arms, changed the universe for ever. Bernard was flat on his back on the bed, an exhausted, monstrous, stillborn child. His hair, just starting to grow back after his treatment, was soft like an infant. His irradiated skin even had the silky sheen of the newly born, as if there was still a promise of a future, a birth not death. I reached out and ran my fingers over the downy hair on his skull. My defeated shrunken brother. And I knew at that moment every breath of my life before had been a lie. The engine would never cough into life. There was no man in a white coat. I was alone. Powerless. Mortal. Standing defenceless beside my dead brother. From the wreckage of Bernard's death cubicle emerged neither brother nor son, just a solitary, vulnerable and very frightened I.

Bernard's death was a hand grenade of rage and grief and love that went off, blasting outwards, everyone falling back, pushing us away from each other. A wound. Somehow, in the hospital, the boy from the island in me asked the matron if she could let Bernard stay in the cubicle so my parents could return to see their dead son by midday. She reluctantly agreed, but her kindness provoked a further intolerable pressure on this unfolding day; a day that by nine in the morning was already one of the worst of my life. Now in the first shock of his death, I knew I had to go home to collect my father and mother and then quickly return. This miserable cubicle, this temporary tomb, was already needed by the press of the living. In my innocence I had blundered into foolishness; there was no space in this besieged ward for time with the dead.

I rushed back to my parents' house into the maelstrom of my keening mother, sisters and Bernard's wife. The immediacy of his death was a convulsion, a physical pain that gripped at your chest, smothering then bursting out in heaving sobs, rivers of tears, panic. The cries of the women, and my own, soared around an ordinary suburban sitting room. The keening was a primeval scream, a calling out of the agony of death, an eruption of despair, tenderness, fear, love, loss and pain. The world sundered around us, broke up and reassembled itself in a savage landscape I could barely recognise. Bernard's wife Marie was wounded. My mother was stricken in grief, temporarily lost. Sonny was caught up in comforting my mother's sorrow. Bernard's death divided us, but there was no time to heal. Bernard was lying dead on a hospital bed and if we wanted to see him we had to leave within minutes.

Someone in the room, I can't remember who, said that we would need to tell the hospital who the family undertaker was when we saw Bernard. I went into the hall by the front door where the old-fashioned telephone directories were kept next to the phone. I started fumbling my way through the yellow pages under 'U' but I felt as if I was scrambling into insanity. The family undertaker? An hour ago, as I walked up those hospital stairs, death had been an abstract concept. But now it seeped through every pore, shuddering through me in terror. I was no more equipped to find the family undertaker than I was to discover the neighbourhood nuclear physicist.

Then someone else called out:

'Try Marino, or Mar . . . something.'

The name seemed Italian, strange for an Irish Catholic family, but I was in no mood to question anything. I soon found the right name amongst the undertaker adverts. There was no one else in the hall. No one else to shoulder the responsibility of making the call. So I did. I dialled the number. The phone rang a couple of times and then a man with a very deep, steady, reassuring voice answered. I told him that my brother Bernard had just died in the hospital and I needed his help. He offered his condolences before saying a few things that I can't remember, checking name spellings, telephone numbers and number of the hospital ward.

'And who should we liaise with in the family about further arrangements?'

I was nineteen and as alone and frightened in that small hallway as you could ever be. With some reluctance, I said: 'Me.'

'That's good, right sir.'

I knew then in this bitter annunciation – in that very moment – in the words of a stranger I had never met – that I was no longer a child or boy, or a student, but a man. A perishable survivor who would bear a mortal responsibility for myself, and others, from that moment onwards to the day, the hour, of my death.

Within minutes, feeling like time was now racing, I was in the car with Sonny heading back towards the hospital. Just the two of us. At Bernard's bedside Sonny stood across from me with his dead son, my dead brother, between us; more equal now than we had ever been. Sonny reached down, kissed his dead boy and stroked his hair. He said a few words – a few phrases, common coinage, about how much he would miss Bernard. Sonny was wounded too, looking aged, heart-struck, vulnerable, a father who had not been able to save this son.

The track of the sun, the coldness of the day and the clear air, sent shafts of sunlight into the room, setting the pink walls aglow, softening the misery of the place. Bernard lay with the sheet up to his chest as if he was sleeping now. The death spasms on his face had calmed, the muscles slackening, receding into the stillness of the sea in the days after a storm in Dookinella. A glass lake. We said goodbye and left him in the hands of the matron, the hospital and the Western Death Machine.

We got in the car and drove slowly back to our city house, passing people doing their shopping, waiting for buses and crossing the road. Curled brown winter leaves blew over their heads, back up through the trees and into the wind beyond before fluttering down somewhere else unseen. The colours through the windscreen seemed so bright, the details achingly vivid and untouchable, as if we were seeing this city, this world, for the first time. As if we were aliens who had just arrived on this other planet identical to Earth, with schoolchildren in uniform, mothers with prams, men in suits, workmen with ladders and cars and shops. And although everything looked the same, in your heart you knew it wasn't. The atmosphere outside the car was toxic, poisonous. If you made the mistake of opening the car window strange gases would kill you. We were trapped.

The air we breathed inside the car was from another world which had broken apart and fallen into meaningless terror. Everything was drenched in death and the pounding heart in your chest felt like it was going to stop beating any second now. And so we drove on in silence until we reached the house, and our keening.

We never had a wake for Bernard; the Machine, the proceedings of dying in the city, the rupture of his death, the defeat of the transplant, had defeated us.

The next time I saw my dead brother was in the funeral parlour. Bernard was dressed in a dark blue suit given to the undertaker as part of the arrangements. The shock of his dead flesh, its chilling coldness, scalded my flesh as if he was as hot as molten lead. I could not believe this human-shaped stone had ever been him.

In the ruins, we did the other things, too; a Mass, a funeral, a trip out to the city crematorium, a few hurried words at the head of the queue of hearses lining up outside, waiting their turn in the allocated slots of that day's burning. Then later we took his ashes home and buried them on Minaun, high up, looking out to the great ocean and to America. We got on with living but it never felt right. Bernard was a wound we never bound up; a grave I could never close.

CHANGELINGS

I became his survivor. My dead brother's changeling. I was plagued by Bernard, alive and dead. Bernard coming home drunk to quell his fear; lying a few feet across from me in the bedroom we had shared; the huge foetal creature in the bed suckling for air from the oxygen mask; still warm in the cubicle; the frigid block in his coffin. Part of me, my bone marrow, had died in his body. But another creature, part of him – a young man who really didn't want to die, who wanted this to stop and fought on so bravely to somehow defeat death – was reborn in me.

I was an angry survivor, enraged against the lies spun about dying. The will to live. You hear that phrase a lot. Those constant 'I'm going to beat this cancer' TV celebrity interviews where the actor/comedian/show-biz personality vows to steadfastly defy their diagnosis. The star's agent assures us this famous so-and-so 'is a real fighter'. Tells of how they never smoked in the first place and have 'such a strong will to live' that a triumphant outcome is not in doubt. As if pap psychology and a 'positive attitude' was a viable defence against cellular mitosis. Death, it seems, is only for quitters and ordinary folk. I was so angry I wanted to smash the television. How much of a 'will to live' was needed to qualify for a rosy future if my dead brother's torment, the sacrifices and agony, was not enough?

Newspapers fill columns with triumphant cancer survivor stories. No one writes about the non-survivors who fill the other columns of the annual mortality statistics. The ninety-nine who die to make the one hero survivor possible. The common dead who disappear as if they were failures who never longed hard enough. Blanked.

In our fear we falsify the inevitable, we deny our nature. Sometimes, for understandable reasons, we fall back on God, or magic, to help us rewrite the reality we cannot bear to face. We turn to Chinese herbs, macrobiotic diets, juicers, the worship of idols or vitamin pills to defeat our own cellular rebellion. We turn to textbooks, to science. We ransack the internet, as if knowledge of an overwhelming enemy was enough in itself to defeat its power.

A few months after Bernard's death, I asked my doctor brother if *being a fighter* or having *a strong will to live* had ever made any difference to the hundreds of patients he had treated for leukaemia. 'No, they all die,' he said, in a voice so devoid of pity or hope, I was too embarrassed to ask any more questions.

For months, years after Bernard, I suffered from his mortality. I imagined every bump on my skin, every cough, was the onset of some crippling cancer that would eat its way out through my guts. I was full of fear. I had, as we like to describe it, an irrational fear of death.

It is hard to explain, but I felt both guilty and glad about Bernard's death. Uneasy thoughts. Bernard never gave his life for me, but my manhood, a mortal survivor, began at the moment of his death. I have had many of the things my dead brother would have wanted: a longer life, a career, more children, a family. I was, and am, selfishly glad it was him not me. But I mourn my dead brother who lost everything. He died, I survived. I won, he lost. I even used Bernard like a lure to make my own life more interesting. I talked about him to lovers. I showed the scars of my bone marrow donation to my partner on the very first night we slept together. I must have thought it made me more sexually attractive. I was the boastful survivor of a distant war in another country, the land of death.

DRIFTS

Bernard's death spilled into me. I felt drawn towards something I still cannot define: human sorrow, lives taken, grief, the mortal aftermath and the realm of the dead. Hades. I drifted into working as a reporter when Ireland's Troubles were still raging and violent death a commonplace. I went in search of a war because I thought I would find the thing I needed amongst the wreckage. I wanted to know what it was like to live on with the memory of the dead, and their dying, inside you, and Ulster was the closest place I could find. I was grieving. Not for my dead brother but for the young man who died with him and lost his mortal innocence. Me.

Ireland is a small country, but Northern Ireland remained a place apart; a battleground of urban tribal enclaves, random sectarian killings, attack helicopters, guns and armoured vehicles, medieval-style British Army castles and pathological hatreds. Maybe it was a child's memory – the frozen violence of flags and emblems, the crouching, nervy camouflaged British soldiers lurking in border hedgerows on the other side of the van window – that also drew me on to Ulster. But

I brought my own baggage. All the stories I reported had a common theme: dead IRA sons, dead bomb-making daughters, dead policemen, dead children and dead brothers. I became too adept at turning up at strangers' doors, inviting myself in, getting them to turn the afternoon horseracing off and asking straight out about their murdered son, their lost daughter. I developed an acute and dangerous gift, and soon I was better at talking about dead strangers than running my own life.

Inside the door we'd begin at the beginning. Who the dead person was. Where they went to school. What they were like. Why and how they were killed. I was an exact practitioner and no detail too trivial was beyond my hunger. What was the tune your dead brother Phelim was playing on his accordion in your downstairs kitchen when three masked assassins came through the green lanes of County Tyrone on a winter's evening to kill you but killed your brother instead? What did you feel, Frankie, when you saw the shadow of one of those strangers flit pass a downstairs window and you ran, in fear, to look out your first-floor bedroom window? And when you saw the man wearing a balaclava at the wheel of a strange car in your driveway? What did you think, then, knowing these killers had come for your life? And then again on the stairs as you crouched down with the sound of machine-gun spray echoing up from the kitchen where Phelim, your brother, had been playing that accordion, and was now certainly dying? And what happened next?

I'd sit on the fringed brown sofa, writing it all down in a notebook. Shamelessly cross-checking dates, quotes and where the bullets went in. Asking them to repeat particular details – the accordion tune was 'Dawning of the Day', an old Irish favourite. Asking who told them what and precisely what words were said. Returning again and again to the same wound. Prodding those stolid, troubled faces until I felt I had gotten all I could.

I wanted every grain, the exact intonation, spoken when two IRA men in duffle coats came to the door of Seamus Flood late on a Friday afternoon. There to pronounce a death sentence on his kidnapped son who their IRA bosses had held captive for seven weeks as a suspected informer.

'The night I did get word, a man came to the door. He must have been five foot eleven because I am not that tall myself and there is a double step at our front door. "Seamus Flood?" I answered: "Aye that's right." "Your son, Paddy? He's not coming back. We've got to go." And then they turned and walked away down the path.'

Two hours before, just south of the Irish border, in a makeshift IRA prison seventy miles away, another IRA man had stuck an AK47 at the back of Paddy Flood's head and blown out his brains, plus a few of his teeth, with a single bullet. The killers put a plastic bag over Paddy Flood's head to catch the blood. Then they loaded his body into an old estate car and drove north into the still July afternoon to dump the corpse like a sack of potatoes in a lay-by just inside the Northern Irish border. The IRA's doorstep annunciation to Paddy's father Seamus was a warped quasi-military notification visit; a death call. A brief private warning from his son's murderers, ahead of the impending breaking news reports of a body being found along the border. Public word of Paddy's death would soon be all over the airwaves and a trail of family mourners, and television crews, at the same door.

Seamus knew their word of Paddy 'not coming back' was a biblical curse in the militant republican area of Derry where he and his family lived. Paddy, in death, was now that accursed thing – an IRA informer, a tout, a betrayer of the tribe. There would be no forgiveness. No value in the denial that Paddy was innocent. That this killing was the result of some internal IRA feud. Or the verdict wrong. Seamus and his kith and kin would now, and in succeeding generations to come, be marked out as the father of a tout, the brother of a tout or the daughter of an informer. The Flood family would be shunned, ostracised, denied. Whatever the words of sympathy to their face, behind their backs most of the neighbours in the street, in the shop, at the school gate, would believe that Seamus's son Paddy was rightly murdered by his oldest friends for his betrayal, long after other killings were forgotten. The IRA bullet that killed Paddy would lethally ricochet on through the lives of the entire Flood family, even those as yet unborn.

I watched the quiver of the lip, the cock of the head and Seamus Flood's eyes staring up beyond my head towards the same front door, as if those IRA men were just about to knock and replay the agony. I wanted Seamus, and others like him, to describe in their words the sounds, the colours of grief. I wanted to taste in my mouth the difference between the living and the dead. To rub my hands on the wound. Because in some mixed-up way I thought it would renew my life like a talisman. I needed the shock of death like a drug, an inoculation, to protect myself from everything I saw and felt in my own life. I needed it because my dead brother had revealed death's denial to be a lie.

We celebrate individualism. It is one of our most cherished values. But when you listen to the radio, the TV, witness the chatter on the internet or between your friends, does it ever begin to sound like the same repeated song? How often do you catch yourself feeling like your life is a play where all the roles – boyfriend, girlfriend, student, best friend, mother, daughter, father, son – are cast from the same pool of character actors? How easy would it be to slip offstage, raid the dressing rooms and slide on the costume of your neighbour three doors along, two work cubicles away or five feet across the bar? How much of your life is you? How much are we – you and me – like the mortal armies of the First World War, with their different little cap badges, languages, uniforms and certainties, caught up in the lies and propaganda of the time, believing in the same empty vanities? Trapped in the same crush of volunteers marching happily up to the front ready for the slaughter? Ending up as just a list of names – and ranks – on a white sandstone memorial. A prop for another empty ceremonial on how great the sacrifice was for a cause even historians have a hard time explaining. Another generation whose lives were lost as casually as a summer's leaves, falling, falling, whirling away into nothingness.

In Flanders' fields nothing remains of the fury for which all those young men, British, German, French, gave their lives, except their own gravestones. Every battlefield, every 'strategic' objective they fought for is another baffling placid field of rolling French countryside indistinguishable from any other. Hunting the landscape of their war is like searching for a mirage. It is so easy to condemn those soldiers' deaths as pointless, but after Bernard I wasn't sure if the lives I saw around me, if my life, was any different. How quickly could we exchange their empty epithet of 'For King and Country' with our own mantra 'For Consumerism and Capitalism' and add to the endless body count?

At least with the dead's relatives I knew where I stood. I could calibrate the value of a life in the wreckage left behind. How the eyes of the living glanced involuntarily to the absence of what was; between a picture of their smiling innocent gunman boy on the mantelpiece and the empty oblong space next to the kitchen counter where their Joseph had lain in his coffin on his last night at home. In the way they rolled the vowels of the name of the dead in their mouths as if soothing a fretful child. In the silences of guilt, in their anger and their soft, irrevocable despair. In the boasts of a broken father, a tailor, sobbing for his murdered boy – blasted to pieces in an IRA bomb in a London street – lamenting how his dead Philip had always carried a good suit well, and danced at Oxford University with the Queen of England's sister, Princess Margaret. As if these fairy-tale words could change or alter or overcome the abyss of Philip's deadness. And I saw the longing too in his eyes for it to be me – an ambassador of the accursed Irish race who had killed his son – to have died by that bomb instead.

In Gaza, I met another father who yearned like the Trojan king Priam for the heart-comforting return of his dead child's body, even though that son, Tariq, had blown himself to fragments with a suicide bomb. Tariq had driven an explosive-packed jeep into an Israeli settlement in Gaza and blew himself up trying, but failing, to kill Israeli soldiers. The immense explosion, the moment of his death, was filmed by his companions and viewed on YouTube a million times in a macabre glorification of his sacrifice. But beyond the propaganda, Diab Hamid's hunger to physically recover the remains of his cherished dead boy for proper burial remained unquenched.

I tracked down mothers whose estranged husbands had gassed their children in the family car and heard the anguish uncoil frame by frame. How he stole her babies and then phoned to taunt her how she would never see them again. How her knees went and she felt sick when the policeman came with a social worker late at night to say the children were dead. How the policemen then drove her 180 miles that night to a morgue where the children lay untouched on a slab, as if perfectly asleep under the covers. So perfectly asleep she was sure she could see them breathing. And could have woken them back up into life if only the morgue officials allowed her to call out to them, touch them, instead of imprisoning her babies behind the glass. How she was trapped in the same dream, manically corkscrewing in a circular car park ramp, tyres screaming, unable to see the driver's face or turn around as the heads of her children appeared on the car's rear shelf calling out to her again and again for comfort.

I listened and listened until I lost count of all the misery I heard.

HADES

The dead in the city dwell in a separate realm from us. Spirited away from their dying places in ambulances, housed in mortuaries, dissected behind closed doors, passed along in black unmarked vans to undertakers, encoffined, buried or burnt unseen. Disappeared.

Warm-blooded, you can sue a policeman for wrongful arrest or invoke the laws of trespass to order council officials off your lawn. Cold-blooded, a state pathologist can, without sanction, gut you from neck to crotch, saw off the top of your skull and pull your brain out for dicing. The dead being dead have no right to challenge the state's dominion, the desecration, of their body. Nor do their living relatives. It is an odd transgression of the sacred Western laws of property. Whose mother, whose body, whose corpse, whose mourning is this anyway?

Our forefathers would be ashamed of us. In the *Iliad*, the Greek hero Achilles kills the Trojan prince, Hector, in revenge for Hector's killing of Achilles' lover, Patroclus, in battle. The mortal clash between the Greek and Trojan champions is the martial and moral centre of Homer's heroic epic of war, courage and destiny. After

125

killing Hector in combat, Achilles pierces his Trojan enemy's heels with his dagger, threads a rope through the flesh and drags Hector's body away behind his chariot. In the Greek camp he allows common soldiers to abuse Hector's corpse and dogs to scavenge on the remains.

Achilles' abuse of Hector's body, his inhumanity, appals the Gods. Zeus intervenes to engineer the return of Hector to Troy for proper burial. In an act of mercy, Apollo, the Lord of Light, masks the wounds inflicted on Hector's mutilated corpse, so his wife and family can see and touch him at his wake. Under the protection of Zeus, Hector's father, Priam, goes alone into the Greek camp to ransom his son's body.

'If it be my fate to die at the ships of the Achæans even so would I have it; let Achilles slay me, if I may but first have taken my son in my arms and mourned him to my heart's comforting.'

Hector's death is a catastrophe for the Trojans, a portent of the fall of the city and their future annihilation. But even in this terror, Priam risks his own life for the love of his son and his duty towards Hector's body.

In our Whisper Death World we have lost any commitment to the bodies of our dead. In the West, we unquestioningly accept the state's removal and butchering of our dead as a high mark of our civilisation, mistaking mundane bureaucracy for existential insurance. The realm of the unseen dead is already beyond us. Death is a job for the Public Health Authorities and a caste of medical professionals, mortuary attendants, undertakers to legislate and regulate, fill in the forms, and clear up the mess. And by some unexplained necessity protect us all, the living and the dead, from something. There must surely be a good reason for this?

Strange diseases?

Potential homicides?

The contamination of the public water supply?

When confronted by the dead we have been trained to call the authorities for 'help'. And what's the alternative? We don't 'do' the dead ourselves any more than we do private rocket trips to the Moon.

Wash, touch, smell?

Do Your Own Dead?

How could you?

Between the dying and disposal, the dead of the city enter a modern Hades, a perfect unchallenged communism, where permission must be asked from minor officials, and can be denied – for even a sight or touch – of your beloved.

We wouldn't advise . . .

It's not usual . . .

I'd better ask . . .

Bodies are taken hostage by the 'authorities' to await lawful release and an allotted slot in the queue for burning at the local council-run crematorium. Dull bureaucracy trumps death's dominion; it can take two weeks to bury your mother. If you don't believe me just try asking for your dead grandfather's body back from the hospital mortuary without the right forms from the right undertaker. The mortuary will never release his body. You are not qualified to deal with the dead. But if grief, love and shared DNA don't qualify you to claim your beloved's body, then what does? Who are these casual strangers to decide what is your heart's comforting?

Death in the West is a mystery that must be answered by a precise matrix of medical subcategories, coronaries, cancers, answers to a worthless question.

What exactly did your grandfather die of?

But what is the 'public interest' in your dead grandfather? Will the delineation of a precise cause on his death certificate bring further 'closure' or reconfigure the mortal coil? We denature nature for what real purpose? Besides the rarity of homicide, suicide and preventable industrial accidents, don't we die of death every day anyway? We are shifting responsibilities not mortalities.

It happened to my mother once, on the sofa in the same front room where we keened over the dead Bernard. She quietly died of a heart attack with a cup of tea and a biscuit on a sunny May morning. Then the ambulance crew who came to save her life, and failed through no fault of their own because she was already dead, hijacked her body for a compulsory post-mortem, chopping her to bits to find a cause before she was put back together for us. Everyone did their day job, but it's hard to believe how you could devise a system more cruel to the bereaved; first the shock of sudden death and then, the body, their body, disappears too. Just so you know who is really in charge here.

Sonny loved my mother and so did her children. It was hard for him, coming in alone from doing a bit of gardening at the front of the house on an ordinary day, to find his wife dead on the sofa. Hard, too, to endure the sight and sound of the ambulance crew zapping and pummelling her body on the sitting room floor in a mandated but fruitless attempt to re-engender. Sonny knew my mother was already dead and told the crew. The crew must have known as well, but could not disobey their mandated instructions – only 8 per cent of all CPR attempts outside a hospital are successful.

Harder still were the actions of these same strangers in stealing our dead mother's body away in the ambulance in which they had arrived sixty minutes earlier. Dead, gone and disappeared in one hour, after forty years of marriage. After a few days, an undertaker was allowed to pick up our mother on our behalf, like freight from the human pound, the city morgue. The next and last time we saw her was somewhere between nine and five in a back room of that now familiar undertaker's parlour. For the sake of our feelings he kept the lighting low and carefully arranged a mantilla veil around my mother's head and neck to disguise the banded shoe lace post-mortem stitches where the top of her skull had been sawn off, sewn up and reassembled.

It is a question worth asking again.

Whose mother was she anyway?

And to whom did her body belong?

Sixty-four, and a couple of stone overweight, my mother, Mary Gallagher, got slotted into the yearly statistics along with the 8,000 other women who died that year of coronary heart failure. What real purpose did her post-mortem serve? Did the exactitude on the death certificate, the validation of the absence of suspicion of homicide and her placing amongst the thousands of commonplace dead, justify the cutting of so many guts? How strange the effort into dismemberment after, and so little into prevention before? Public policy on saturated fats and tobacco sales remained unchanged. As did the following year's mortality figures, apart from an added digit. Whoever even reads the post-mortem reports of the common dead? Who exactly benefits? Not the corpse, for sure.

Like Odysseus, I volunteered for Hades and entered the forbidden realm of the city dead. I wanted to unshield myself from every disguising of the Western Death Machine. I wanted to cross over the urban Styx and see what had happened to my mother. In the mortuary of a city of half a million, I watched the flow of the ordinary dead arrive – haphazard packages waylaid in transit – to be sliced, sawed, diced and replumbed back together.

We die at the rate of 1 per cent a year. Half a million divided by a hundred equals 5,000 dead citizens a year, of whom roughly 800 are post-mortemed because their deaths, like my mother's, were not deemed entirely predictable. Strokes, heart attacks, suicides and happenstances arrived on the slab at a rate of two or three a day, except at weekends when numbers rose due to family gatherings, feuds, binge drinking or drugs sessions gone wrong. Old folks' summer coach trips, winter flu epidemics and Christmas drinks parties played havoc with supply, a surfeit of the dead, but even in between the constancy never ceased. A naked old lady who had slipped away in the night after a bowls matches, and, judging by her stomach contents, a beef Madras curry. Mesothelioma victims with stony asbestos fibre-encrusted lungs that had to be ripped away from their carcase; their disease a biological chronicle of the city's industrial past.

An aged grandmother whose post-operative blood pressure levels had precipitately leapt beyond control, bursting the sutures on her aortic valve replacement surgery, hosing her chest cavity with free-flowing blood like a burst tyre. In vain her surgeon had reperformed open heart surgery on the open ward to stem the wound. And then amidst the panic, the unceasing spray, the litres and litres of plasma and platelets, the surgical teams, the frantic effort and growing blood-bath on the floor, proclaimed out loud: 'I don't think this is working.'

And stopped trying to stop her dying. Gone.

Beyond the threshold of the mortuary loading dock, it was easy to see these unconnected dead as Other. Them. Perhaps it was necessary. In an antechamber, a bit like a school changing room, you took off your outside clothes, stripped down to t-shirt and shorts, changed into a medical gown, found the right sized yellow wellingtons, opened the examining room door and entered the land of the dead; the tiles, concrete and the drains for the blood in the floor. There was a vinegary blood smell, a bowelly meatiness, in the air. Hard to exactly classify; the whiff of raw meat too long in the fridge but easily bearable. After the morning's cutting, we went to the canteen for tea and biscuits and talked about cars, houses and lots of other forgettable things. Another day in Deathland.

Along with the coronaries and brain-bleeding strokes came the reckless and Unlucky young. A tattooed and shell-suited novice druggie, his shaven head like a golden eggshell, whose possibly first but definitely last heroin injection had ended all future adventure; a fool or carefree soul whose druggie companions had first helped him to inject, panicked at his heart-spasming opiate shock, and then delayed – to hide the evidence – before calling an ambulance. The ambulance crew, according to the notes, had, klaxons blaring, tyres screeching, tried the last; CPR, intubation, adrenaline, naloxone, whilst delivering their charge to the local Accident and Emergency in time to declare a DOA. A Dead on Arrival. Who lay now on the morgue slab, still intubated, two pipe-like tubes sticking out of his mouth. A crime scene. But otherwise without a mark, as if like an erstwhile football fan he had merely passed out in slumber, in green tracksuit and trainers, after a skinful of cider on a summer's day in a local park. A hapless, now truly carefree, lout.

The twenty-six-year-old woman with learning difficulties, Margaret, who slept around in her circle of equally intellectually challenged male friends and then teased one to the other about the size of his penis. The stung lovers and four other friends combined to beat and strangle their sexual tormentor, before borrowing a supermarket trolley to wheel her body to the local park, hoping no one else would notice. Cut once in the original post-mortem after her body was found, Margaret had to be unpacked all over again, one organ at a time, for the defence post-mortem, after her ex-lovers were charged with murder.

The mortuary was not so very different from an abattoir and the dead, product. Meaty human dolls, to be chopped up and rearranged between 8 a.m. and 2 p.m., Monday to Friday, and only at weekends in an emergency. On top of their salary, each pathologist received a payment for every job, £87 at the time. Piecework, so to speak. If you were a fast cutter, fifty-five minutes head to toe, you could make yourself an extra £400 by lunchtime. Within the morgue's blank walls, mortem was an industrial process devoid either of sentiment or curiosity for the customers' lives before. Happy? Sad? Loved? Today's customers were flesh to be carved, not psychologies to be explored.

On the slab I found it hard not to wonder. Did they struggle in fear of the rib-cloying cancer that pressed down millstone-weight on their lungs? Panic that this heart-gripping vice and the shooting pains in the arm was the Big One? Claw and gag, desperate for air, at the suffocating failure of lungs to rise and draw in breath as their heart fibrillated in shock? Blackout into oblivion even before they hit the floor? Or stumble into inadvertent suicide; running a hot bath for that sensuous post-fix high, whose bubbling waters would overflow, run down the stairs and swirl around inside the locked family front door for hours after. A bath whose possessor ended up here instead – flat out on the slab – after the darkness descended over her eyes. Short, dirty blonde hair, five feet four inches tall, freckled forearms, bitten nails, a smudged butterfly tattoo above her left breast. A 'Sarah', it said on the nametag, a late twenty-something who had fatally administered her end in the bedroom adjacent to the running bath, via a syringe filled with heroin.

Like the other muted dead, Sarah would no longer answer. The sins of failure remained behind written in flesh; the scars of battle, wounds, clogged arteries, brain bleeds, tumours, hidden prick marks, or the toxicology of the drug that ceased them to be. With a stopped heart Sarah's own blood now betrayed her, capturing the moment of death. The skin of her calves was engorged in a purplish hypostasis, where her blood, devoid of pressure, had drained down as she had sat still and dead in the same chair seeking the euphoria that killed her.

Living, we expend our lives lying about something; your mother's love or lack of it, how fat we are or how thin, drink, the porn you watch, the sex you never have, the state of your marriage, the shape of your nose, penis, breasts, your qualifications, job, lovers, friends, your children's exams, the cost of the shopping, money and happiness. The price of face cream. Capitalism depends upon it, for why else would we buy anything shiny or new at all? With the dead alongside, it's hard not to laugh out loud at the flimsiness of our talent for self-deception when we each, in our own way, push the needle in.

The dead being dead lose all power to deceive themselves, and the living. Lying naked before our gaze, the dead are everything and nothing like us; perfect copies but insensible to pain, shame, breath or regret. In their company it is impossible not to grasp the thinness of the perishable gap between ourselves and these cold-blooded not-so-very Others. How easy was it for this sprawling lump of flesh – twenty-two stone with a scrawl of tattoos from shoulder to crotch, nametagged 'Mark' – to believe he could outrun the clock? Or not one day succeed through trying hard, judging by his fatty, frying-pan-sized cirrhosis liver, at drinking himself to death? Unless that was part of the plan?

How long did this mutilated thirty-nine-year-old Eleanor listen to the doctor talk of tests, remissions, chemo, shrinkage, resistance, and metastatic invasion? Stages One to Four? Deceived, as we all might be, into believing life-hopes that further mutate like wayward cells into death-truths.

And how different from your own once bright marital love is the one that ended here with a banal suicide note left dashboard-behind, detailing exact petty sums in wages owing to the nanny and the cleaning lady, whilst their writer went on to shatter all future domestic serenity by gassing herself cherry pink in the family car?

Maybe the suicidal dead never meant to do it? Was it all just a cry for help to break the lonesome silence? Something they never planned to go through with? How many times a day do we, the living, go back on ourselves? Promise to change and ask forgiveness. Vow to never touch another drop. Snort another line. Say cruel things we later say were untrue. Or genuinely retract. Who hasn't ever said or done something we regret? But the suicidal dead, no longer breathing, confound themselves, leaving no future space in which to reverse or apology to offer. However arbitrary their intention, whatever was remains a 'was'; stopped and sundered, absolute, at the moment.

The blonde Sarah who ran but never laid in her bubbling bath had lied, and lied, most often probably to herself, that she was 'clean' and would never use heroin again. Except on this last day when she did. Going into town to sell an old laptop, as agreed with her mother, but flush with extra cash, taking a furtive detour via the local McDonald's where her old dealers hung out to purchase a secret. Looking forward on the bus journey home, with the burning wrap of heroin in her pocket, to what she would do to herself in the still afternoon of her mother's house. Lying to herself now, falling back. Persuading herself, as we all might, that this little lapse, this just-this-once, would never matter since no one else would ever know? Caught out only by the purity of the buy and the abstinence that lowered her opiate tolerance. And so it ends for Sarah; all happy seaside childhood memories, spades and sandcastles and dreams of futures-to-be. Quiet and still on the slab after her butchering, branded by her Y-shaped post-mortem incisions. Ready now to slip down and down and take her place amongst the mouldering weight of the fixed dead, receding in time and distance from us, falling away, sinking slowly, into an ocean of oblivion. Lost.

If it was not so sad it would be funny. Laurel and Hardy. The bath water, foot deep, gushing out in a comic torrent, when Sarah's confused mother returned from work in the evening and opened the front door. What did her mother think had happened, before running up the stair into nightmare?

Perhaps we need to joke out loud to keep our distance in the raw suicidal wash, our futile anguish at such deaths. Laugh, a bit, at Sarah and the Other Wilful Self-Deceased; the bridge-jumpers, train-leapers, car-gassers, gun-to-the-forehead-pointers, and stones-in-their-pockets swimmer-drowners? Maybe we need to. For ourselves. A gleeful, life-affirming, precious comfort to enumerate our separation from such sad, sorry fools. Those Others who readily delve their way to the ever open grave. Purchase inglorious exit with a portion of French fries and a side order of a £10 bag of poison or a simple vault over the barrier at the Golden Gate. Persuade ourselves we could never be them. Until we are.

There was a terrible beauty in the sawing apart, the blood and guts, the engorged flooded lungs, extracted and weighed, 640 grams each, to demonstrate their life-ending opiate spasm. And in the mechanics of the cutting of the flesh. The skin of the face being sliced behind the ears. And then pulled forward and down like an orange rag over the eyes, to reveal a red-smeared gleaming skull, before the whirl of the circular saw rounded out a hollowed crown. As the top of the skull came off there was a little splurge of bloody liquid, brain fluid, and then the prize exhibit – a reddish cod roe brain, exposed, glimmering, ready to be plucked out for inspection. A convoluted greyish portal to a once-was, bearing we think the imprint of every sensation, thought and betrayal, but now no more than tripe to be sliced. Just matter not soul.

After all the organs – kidney, heart, liver – were salami-diced and sampled, the pathologist stuffs the guts rubbish-like into a black plastic bin bag, stuffs the bag into the stomach cavity, packs the empty skull with tissue, replaces the bony crown, pulls the face back in place and stitches everything back up in workmanlike shoelace loops; there being no value in closer wasted effort since these patients neither bleed nor complain. Soon today's dead were reassembled and whole again as if recast. Ready to be showered off, boxed up and returned, mostly unseen, to undertaker parlours, relatives, funerals, the crematorium or a plot in the crowded Victorian necropolises ringing this industrial city. Flowing away into the endless river that runs unseen behind and below us, around and beyond, the urban Styx.

Why then in childish fear and woeful forgetfulness do we shun the dead of our own species and refuse Priam's heart-comforting embrace? The sight and touch of our kin is nothing to be afraid of. Nor to be dreaded. The still dead are our pictures, no longer burthened, but the very best of all mortal reminders of the full transitory measure of being human; lying there lifeless before us, having arrived peremptorily at what will be, whether we deny them or not, our own future designation: Dead on Arrival.

GESTATIONS

Sonny's death took nine months to come into being.

It was in the autumn as Sonny approached his seventieth birthday that he first began to complain of indigestion and a burning pain at the top of this stomach. By Christmas he was in sufficient discomfort to have visited his doctor three times and been sent to the local hospital for tests. The tests came back negative.

I missed his seventieth birthday party that January. My brother and sisters and Sonny's sisters went for a meal in a restaurant on the island. Everyone sang 'Happy Birthday'. They had a birthday cake with candles, and he blew them out. I did not think being there was important. I was living in London; my first child had just been born and we were worried about her. I thought I could not afford the time, the money or the disruption. I knew my presence would have pleased Sonny in his own quiet way. But I never went, persuading myself I would make it up to him sometime in the future. When my mother was alive, Sonny had made his views known through her, but she was gone and he was never a man to demand things openly. It was easy to ignore him. I still regret my thoughtlessness.

I came home in early March to show him his new grandchild. But Sonny was unusually quiet and inactive. He spent a lot of time sitting around watching television. He was preoccupied, hard to read, fallen into himself, a bit cranky. He was due to go for more tests but he never mentioned his symptoms – or perhaps I never listened. We went out for the day, stopping for tea and cakes at the Sisters of Saint Lucy convent in the little town of Newport, where my mother used to buy meat on those long van journeys. Sonny bought his new grandchild a soft felt purple rabbit in the gift shop. We halted near a harbour for a short walk, but Sonny did not want to get out of the car. I passed it off as old age, grumpiness. I took a few photographs by the side of the car; Sonny smiling holding his granddaughter, Sonny and me, Sonny with my partner. We drove back to Dookinella, and then a few days later we flew to the city to get on with the rest of our lives.

Sonny's nagging pain did not disappear, and not long after our visit he had those further tests and an exploratory operation. The surgeon opened him up and found an advanced cancerous tumour in his pancreas. Pancreatic cancer is the seventh most common cancer found in Western men, but is particularly fatal. The survival rate five years after initial diagnosis, even with chemotherapy, is just 5 per cent; after ten years, 1 per cent. The pancreas gland, at the back of the abdominal wall near the top of the stomach, acts like a biological junction between the body's digestive system and bloodstream, controlling digestion through the production of insulin and blood enzymes. Cancerous cells from the tumour rapidly spread to nearby organs via the arteries, just as the tumour's growth blocks vital bile ducts which enable the digestion of food. One of pancreatic cancer's most common symptoms is starvation. Sonny's tumour was inoperable. The surgeon closed the wound and sewed Sonny back up again. The diagnosis was decisive. Sonny was going to die. My father's time had come.

TOMBS

If you stand in the ruins of the old village of Dookinella and look to the north, you can easily see the cluster of graveyards, old and new, on the slopes of Slievemore mountain, where the islanders bury their dead. The oldest inscriptions that can be read date from the mid-1800s, but even these tombs are amongst the youngest on the mountain. Higher up lies a long string of megalithic tombs dating from around 4000 BC. The island, geologists say, was warmer and drier back then, forested, and the mild winters allowed Neolithic farmers to feed their cattle on pasture all year round.

Slievemore was a human burial ground long before we started using metal, and its tombs thousands of years older than our cities of glass and steel. One of the biggest tombs, known as a court tomb, is set almost in the middle of the mountain on the lower slopes and dominates the whole bay, the nearby lake, the shore and the fertile fields between. In front of the tomb are circles of upright stone teeth, thrusting skywards from the green earth forming the court entrance. Beyond this court, towards the ocean, is a large table rock, weighing at least thirty tonnes, carefully set on a base of stone pillars. The table rock, perfectly flat, is big enough for two people to lie on. Its downward edges are recessed and taper away underneath the stone as if carved deliberately, though the Neolithic farmers who erected this grave only had stone tools. The tomb's creation must have been a massive communal enterprise. The stones were dragged down hundreds of metres from the glacial scree, the morass left behind by Ice Age glaciers that covers the upper reaches of Slievemore, and then carefully positioned in the old treeline. Similar Neolithic tombs are scattered across Europe, from Norway to Malta and into Jordan and Syria. No one knows the exact funeral rituals Neolithic people used, but we know the dead were important, given the size of the tombs and the effort of their creation. When excavated, Neolithic tombs often contain the selected bones or cremated remains of many different individuals. Individual tombs are also known to have been in use for as long as 600 years. The tomb on Slievemore, on the far western reaches of Europe, marks the furthest boundary of that Neolithic world and those forgotten faiths.

In 1897, an English traveller stumbled upon a funeral procession descending Minaun and heading towards Slievemore.

I saw a singular procession winding sinuously down the opposite cliff. Men and women on horseback, the men attired in the conventional costume of the Irish high holiday, to wit, tall hats, breeches, and dress cut coats of thick frieze; the women barefoot as usual, but with feet well washed, the short red kirtle reaching to the knee, the head and shoulders swathed in brilliant-coloured shawls, the man astride in front, the woman balancing herself astride the crupper, all riding bare-backed, all guiding their yellowish steeds by means of a bridle of plaited straw. Sometimes there were three on a horse, never less than two. And there might be fifty horse proceeding at a slow pace, accompanied by some fifty woman on foot. In the middle of the funeral train was one of the flat carts used in Connaught with the humble coffin of unplaned wood and two women sitting on top. A poor woman had lost her son by drowning in Blacksod Bay and occupied this position, accompanied by her daughter, a good-looking girl of twenty or so . . . On went the strange procession of the long line of riders, with the tanned complexions of the women, their jet black hair, their naked limbs dangling in the horses' flanks, and the bright colours of their attire. Here and there isolated dwellers in the villages lying on the route emerged on horseback, with the invariable 'God be with you' in Irish, to which came the invariable reply 'God and the Virgin be with you.' The way was long, but at last the cortege turned sharply to the right towards a hamlet on the mountainside. Somewhat short of it was a rudely-walled enclosure, without any chapel, lych-gate, or shelter of any kind, a wilderness of dense-growing nettles, among which the bare-footed women walked and pushed their way with profound indifference to the stings, each lifting her voice in the Irish wail at the moment the coffin passed the graveyard wall. Echoing up the mountain, resounding over the lake hard by, never surely was heard a more fearsome chant. Beginning on a high note, the voices descended together in a sort of chromatic scale, not unlike the cry of a starling at certain seasons, the chorus numbering by this time at least a hundred women whose lungs equalled their enthusiasm, the men remaining silent placing the coffin by the family grave and waiting until prescriptive custom brought their turn to act. Presently the 'keen' subsided, and the crowd dispersed among the graves, many throwing themselves at full length among the nettles and clasping the poor mound in an agony of grief, kissing it and calling in heart-broken accents to the dead, with many bitter tears. Meanwhile two young fellows were digging the grave, the widow and her daughter sitting on the coffin a yard away, and watching every stroke.

'Keening', women openly lamenting the dead, singing in unison around the dying and the dead, is as old as the megalithic tombs on Slievemore, as old as the ancient Greeks, the Celts, maybe as old as the human story itself.

In the Book of Jeremiah, 17:20, in the Old Testament, written in the sixth century BCE, the Prophet, denouncing the idolatry of his fellow Jews, cries out in lament over the impending destruction of Jerusalem.

Call for the wailing women, that they may come, and send for the most skilful of them. Let them make haste and take up a wail for us, that our eyes may run down with tears, and our eyelids gush with water. For a voice of wailing is heard out of Zion. How we are spoiled and confounded because we have forsaken the land. You hear the word of the LORD. O ye women let your ear receive the word of his mouth and teach your daughters wailing, and every one her neighbour lamentation.

In the New Testament, Luke 23:28, Jesus Christ encounters the professional wailing daughters of Jerusalem on his way to Calvary and tells them not to weep for him but for themselves. It was a foretaste of Christianity's unremitting hostility to the pagan rituals of waking the dead. St Paul's First Letter to the Thessalonians, AD 51, was the first of many denunciations of wakes as 'devilish in origin'.

Despite such strictures, waking and keening over

the corpse remained common throughout Europe up to the nineteenth century until death itself began to be silenced. But out in the far west, in Ireland, on the island, amidst the Celts, the wake did not die as the English travellers, Mr and Mrs S.C. Hall, who visited the island in the 1830s, witnessed.

> The women of the household range themselves on either side of the corpse and the keen (*caoine*) commences. They rise with one accord, and, moving their bodies in slow motion to and fro, their arms apart, they keep up a heart-rending cry. The cry is interrupted for a while to give the *bean chaointe* an opportunity of commencing. At the close of every stanza of the dirge, the cry is repeated, to fill up, as it were, the pause, and then dropped; the woman, the *bean chaointe*, then again proceeds with the dirge, and so on to the close.

The death rituals the Halls describe are no different from those described at Hector's wake; the keening, the grieving of close female relatives, lighted tapers beside the corpse, guarding the body through the night, the gathering and the feasting. Neither the poet Homer, the ancient Greeks, nor the Prophets saw any shame in public sorrow. And nor would the islanders at Sonny's coming wake.

GATHERINGS

Dying is not an act you can easily undertake yourself. If being born amidst those who will love you is the first best hope of life, dying *within* a community is the last. Sonny knew he needed help. You need help from a midwife, a *bean chabrach* for the journey through your dying into death. You need advice about what to do next, when to let go, and someone other than yourself to manage the loss of powers. Sonny placed his trust in his youngest child Teresa, to whom he had grown very close, to help him make the big decisions and take responsibility for those he could no longer accomplish. Teresa in turn would take advice from our *bean chaointe*, Aunt Tilda, who passed on all she had learnt from Mariah, her grandmother; the chain of the wake, the pathway to death, and the knowledge of the wake's rituals reaching far back in time.

Sonny would not have an easy death. Pancreatic cancer has a catastrophic effect on the body's digestive system. As secondary cancers spread through his body, the tumour partially blocked Sonny's intestine and gave food a sharp, unpalatable, metallic taste. Eating became an ordeal. He vomited up almost everything he ate. Sonny, always a physically powerful man, rapidly began to lose weight and grow frail. His days shoring along the cliffs underneath Minaun with Darcy, or tending to his garden, were over. His physical world dwindled to two rooms; his stark white-washed bedroom and the adjacent sitting room. Sonny knew he would not see the summer's hay being saved or the turf coming down from the bog by tractor and trailer-load in the long evenings when the last of the western light still gleamed in the sky past midnight. Sonny had weeks not months to live.

The biggest decision of Sonny's life came soon after his operation. The nuns from a local convent on the island offered to help with Sonny's nutrition, feeding him through a nasal tube in their small community hospice a few miles away. The nasal feeding tube would bypass the expanding blockage in his digestive system and the additional nutrition would extend his life. Inevitably, he would become the nuns' full-time patient and die there in their convent. Sonny did not want to leave Dookinella, but he was unsure. So one morning Sonny and Teresa sat down together at the kitchen table, looking out over the strand and the waves, and talked. Sonny did not want to die. If the nuns could have made Sonny better, then he would have gone to the hospice. But both Teresa and Sonny accepted that the feeding tube could only prolong his life by a few weeks.

What kind of a life is this to preserve?

Neither Teresa nor Sonny gave an answer to the question, but the pathway to his death was now clear. Sonny would die at home, the circle of his life finishing in the same village where it had begun seven decades ago, and within sight of the same drystone house in the old village, now a ruin, where he had been born. Once they had decided Sonny wasn't going anywhere, things somehow relaxed. It was like a huge weight of responsibility had been taken off Sonny's shoulders, Teresa said.

Sonny neither clung to life nor sought to hasten his end. He was not brave or heroic or defiant, but something rarer, wiser; he was accepting. He determinedly got on with dying the same way he had got on with living. He preserved his energy for the time he had left and stood ready on shore as if waiting for the incoming tide to engulf him. He made a will, paid his debts and settled his estate. As his parting gift, he ordered a fancy electric sheep shearer from England for his old friend Mikey, one of the village shepherds, and worried that it would not arrive before his death. The local doctors helped, supplying a special mattress to prevent bedsores, drugs to treat the symptoms and a morphine pump to ease the pain. Teresa, still recovering from the birth of her daughter, installed the baby monitor in Sonny's room in case he needed her in the night.

But as Sonny weakened that early summer, something different from the Anglo-Saxon way of death began to happen; the house filled with people. Rather than shun him, people came to see Sonny specifically *because* he was dying. The doorbell rang and rang. His sisters, neighbours, cousins, old schoolmates from sixty years before, even strangers, made their way to Dookinella. Often there would be a queue of visitors, like supplicants, waiting for Sonny to emerge from his bedroom in the late morning. Some visitors, his sisters and close neighbours, would be admitted to sit by his bedside if he was too tired to get up. Others he avoided. What did they chat about? What do you say to a dying man? Within the Irish Wake the answer is simple. Sonny's visitors spoke to him in his sickness as they would have spoken to him in health. They talked together about his illness, the past, the weather, the price of land, of his and their childhood, and the latest minor political scandal. The shutters that divide the Western world, between the living us and the dying them, were not there. Not all of these conversations were easy and some questions had an absurd ring.

Are you feeling any better today?

You should eat to keep your strength up?

There were inevitably awkward moments, but for his visitors this was their last chance to speak with a man they had known for decades. When else could they do so? Sonny's wake, his community's and his own acceptance of his dying had already begun. His visitors had come to say goodbye.

Sonny was dying but he was never alone. The gathering allowed Sonny to call upon his family and his friends if he wanted company, and to ignore them if he wanted to sleep. He had good days and bad days as he weakened. Sometimes he was weary and the pain too intrusive. Some visitors bored or tired Sonny and he retreated to bed. He had loved my mother, missed her, and drew comfort from the hope of heaven and their being reunited in an afterlife.

Sonny never flinched. He talked to Teresa about where his coffin would lie in the sitting room and what it would be like to lie within it, being stared at dead. One day, a distant relation came to visit. It was a final parting. Thomas was emigrating to Australia in the next couple of weeks and Sonny's time was shortening. The two men chatted in Sonny's room for half an hour. As he was leaving, Thomas casually said:

'I'll be seeing you, Sonny.'

'Not in this life, Thomas, not in this life,' Sonny replied.

Outside the room the bulky builder, a man in his fifties, burst into tears.

At other times, Sonny was afraid. One night Teresa went out for a drink, leaving Sonny watching television in the care of a cousin. Teresa was not long in the bar when she received an emergency call and rushed back. Sonny was on the sofa frightened, his pulse racing and his breathing rapid. He had stood up to go to the toilet, but on his feet felt dizzy and staggered. He nearly passed out. It was probably tiredness or hunger; he hadn't been able to eat much that day. But as he swayed in his carpet slippers beside the turf fire and the television, Sonny thought he was dying and he called out in fear for Teresa. Sonny was afraid, not of dying, but of dying unexpectedly, and of dying unprepared. The dizzy spell passed, it was nothing.

I came home to see him long and gaunt in his deathbed, his skin darkening from the jaundice of his failing liver and the secondary cancers that nestled there. He was already impossibly thin; shedding powers like a snake sheds skin. Dying was his job now and it consumed most of his energy. His days were spent in bed, propped up on the pillows, his mind and body closing on the final gateway. One morning, I took my six-month-old daughter Storme into the room and she reached out and touched Sonny's arm as it lay on the bed, reaching across the space of three human generations; one life ending, another beginning, just as Homer had written in the *Iliad*. Sonny was sleeping and never woke up.

I was with my father for less than a week. I had for some reason to return to the city, for something I felt was too important to delay, so important that I have entirely forgotten what it was. It was my time to say goodbye to my father. Sonny was still in his room resting in his bed, his left arm attached to a drip that now fed a constant dribble of morphine into his veins to dampen the growing pain. The morphine made him sleepy, but his mind when he woke was sharp and clear. The biggest change of all in his body was not the savage weight loss but his hands. All my life Sonny's hands, his tools, had been so deeply ingrained with oil and dirt that no amount of scrubbing could entirely remove the dark streaks from the rough leathery cracks in his fingers. Now his hands, puffy with excess body fluid, were soft and pink. As I held his left hand between my own, I told him how strange it was to see his hands so clean.

'I'd rather they were dirty, Kevin, than here in this bed and clean.'

It was the only time I ever heard regret in Sonny's voice. I asked him if he was afraid of dying.

'Not at all. If there were in this life a choice of when to die then I would choose to die later. But there is no choice. And so I must die soon.'

Our last living words to each other were banal, very ordinary. I told Sonny I was going. We both foresaw this was probably our final parting. I gave him a hug and kissed him.

'I'll let you go now, son. All the best, lad.'

I did not break away in tears. Neither did Sonny.

Dying is a self-centring act. Sonny was busy now with his own impending death. There was no more meaning to give, no revelation to share and no space left for the burdens of the living or their responsibilities. Our past, the mystery, as father and son, was already written out in all the commonplaces of our lives; Sonny changing my nappy, dressing me for school, praising or castigating me in adolescence; in the summers we shared as I worked as a labourer with him on building sites, and in all the countless ways he showed me in his craft how to be a man and a father myself. The baggage of our past had already been passed on, transmuted into my life and the lives of my children to come. His fatherhood would frame my own future fatherhood as his own father must have framed his. Whenever I reach for a tool, a hammer, a screwdriver, or ask my teenage son to hold a piece of wood or metal as I screw the other end down, Sonny's shadow is always with me. But even on his deathbed, Sonny was still my teacher. In those final days he was showing his children, and his community, the last parental lesson of all. How to die.

FOREBODINGS

The sadness I saw and heard as a reporter filled me with a kind of light. It felt easier to live with death close, than to live with the emptiness of denial. I wanted to, felt the need to, be a witness. In death's true nature there could be no illusions, no fooling yourself with false comfort. I thought I was going forward, gathering secrets, clues, in the way I still gathered stones on the beach at Minaun. As if each sliver of a death I captured was another piece of armour I could pin on to grow a new skin. Forge a weapon to face my own life, and my own death. But every notebook I filled came with a price, a fingertip bruise on the arm that never healed, a mark. The gift of being able to talk my way over a stranger's threshold and within minutes ask about the worst moments of their lives also left me raw and un-protected against what I heard.

I got some of what I wanted, the elixir of grief, but the words began to sting like acid on the skin. My dreams began to conjure the dead. The lost lives described by those I interrogated returned as compulsive ghosts, in-truders, no longer silenced; murdered prostitutes, dead boys, missing girls. Fragments from a discordant past tumbled into the present – the siren words of long-dead strangers echoed back by those who now sat opposite me on the sofa. Each new encounter began to feel like a returning step on the same winding stair.

The sadness I had sought had taken separate form and could play itself out again inside my mind against my will. I began to know too much about other worlds, other lives – negation – where the cruellest possibilities in human nature reigned and everyone died alone in terror. And there was no stop button. The worst, worst movies in the world.

I began to believe inside myself I would come to harm, take a bullet, somewhere on the road. A foreboding. I expected it though I told no one. I was so filled up with death that my own must be ordained somewhere in the coming months, prescribed in stone; in a chaotic moment, the wrong turn in a 'safe' suburb in a town I had never heard of, a chance encounter with gunmen who really were after someone or something else.

For a decade I travelled a lot; Jerusalem, Beirut, Damascus, Kabul, Quetta, Teheran, Gaza, the Bekaa Valley, Jenin, Nablus, Islamabad and in between. I became an expert on terrorism and suicide bombing. I made films and wrote stories. I had adventures. I crossed through tribal badlands disguised as a woman, dressed up in a burka, to avoid discovery. I went to the funerals of dead martyrs; talked to soldiers whose skin was still pitted with the shrapnel of their attackers; knocked on doors of the families of suicide bombers in small towns on the West Bank; spent time in Israeli prisons talking to failed suicide bombers; and drove around in the green valleys of Lebanon and Afghanistan, full of ancient ruins, where you stood a reasonable chance of being taken hostage or murdered just because you were a foreigner.

No one forced me, I volunteered. I was not brave or reckless. I did not want to get shot, but I had a gift. I could talk my way, with my camera crew, through all manner of closed doors, and it was exciting, fulfilling. I was always good at asking awkward, never-asked questions.

What was it like when you first tried on the suicide bomb vest?

And when you shot him did he say anything?

After they had murdered your son and showed you his body what did you do?

How many people do you think you murdered with that car bomb?

This was my life now; a journalistic soldier, more sergeant than general. A lone wolf who roved without a home, or much regard from those who employed me, but more committed than anyone else; the only one left behind on watch when everyone else had sensibly gone home. I really did want to know why your twenty-nine-year-old daughter, who smiled shyly like a teenage girl in her prerecorded martyrdom video, strapped on a suicide bomb vest and went to the grill restaurant to murder twenty-one people. Ordering a chicken kebab, waiting forty-five minutes for the dining room to fill, before standing up, walking to the middle of the most crowded section, close to whole families dining together on humus, kebabs and salads, and pressing the detonator that blew her body apart from neck to legs. As the shrapnel, like machine-gun spray bursting out from her stomach, tore through surrounding bodies, killing children, mothers, fathers, grandmothers, grandfathers. A deathly ravishment that turned a casual lazy *Shabbat* gathering into the horror of a funereal feast, stranding the dead upright in their seats at the same table where they ate. Whilst on the floor at their feet, decapitated in the blast, lay the bodiless head of their murderess.

Naively, I thought knowing the truth of these things would make me a better person. I felt it was my duty to know everything, to talk to the witnesses, mull over forensic photos and find a reason why this woman had blown herself up. The answer was that an Israeli assassination squad had murdered the bomber's fiancé and younger brother on the family doorstep six months earlier. The question I could never really answer was, why did I still want to know? More knowing, uncovering a pitiable truth behind her actions, didn't change the cruelty of the act. The understanding gave me more understanding of other shattered lives, the circles of motivation, but brought me no closer to understanding myself.

On the road I was most often alone. I stumbled back on the same tricks, moves and lies I had known twenty years before. It felt as if I was condemned to replay a variant of the same script, catching myself mouthing the same lines, easing myself into the room over the doorstep, sitting back down on the same sort of sofa, the decor changed, but otherwise all the roles identical to those undertaken before in Ireland's Troubles. I went on anyway, journeying the same road, trapped. By now I was not qualified to do anything else.

I met and talked with a lot of people who had a lot of other people's blood on their hands; assassins, Lebanese torturers, mass killers, car bombers, cold-blooded Israeli intelligence chiefs, blind fanatics, war criminals who slaughtered thousands and ordinary everyday murderers. In secret police headquarters in places like Kabul, I interviewed men who ached to kill me and everyone in the room – by pressing the button on their suicide belt right at that moment if they could – except for the fortunate circumstance that they were prisoners and disarmed.

I wasn't careless with my life but I thought I had run out of chances, and maybe I deserved it. 'Deserved' is probably the wrong word but it did feel like fate. The more you spin the wheel, the more you risk the moment coming when all the odds spin wrong. And I couldn't think of a good reason why it should not happen. One minute you're safe in a mud-walled hotel in a nervy town on a bad highway running to nowhere, and the next minute a local warlord and a platoon of peasant gunmen have arrived to kidnap you. I was not part of some big organisation that would send in the marines if anything went wrong. I was on my own, a hired subcontractor. Most of the time it was just me and the local translator. Or I was with a small team and I was responsible for their lives too.

I knew my death wouldn't be personal. I wasn't that important. It would be a minor futility. Other colleagues, friends, had met the same fate; shot dead by assassins, killed in traffic accidents, crashed in aeroplanes. Some had died innocently of cancer or after being flung head first over the handlebars of their pushbike on a peaceful country lane, after their return from risky assignments in dodgy places. I had stood in the line beside them, crossing through the same awkward checkpoints, at the same time. Walked up in fear towards the same doorway on the same job. Worried that I was leading them into danger. Awkwardly, and uselessly, tamped down my fear of getting blown up by a landmine by squirming on the hard car seat but saying nothing. Sat opposite them, envious of their worldly success, in a bar. Ate at their table and carried their coffin on my shoulders to the grave.

Once you start seeing how easily other people get killed for no good reason there is no other good reason to believe why you shouldn't be killed, too. Death, I knew now, could happen anywhere. Inside, I knew the only thing between me and death now was chance – seat 42C not 39A. I kept travelling, but as I sat down on the outbound aircraft seat I always thought: 'Will this be the one? The journey where that bullet at last catches up to me?'

After a time, I stopped going away to other people's wars. Like the Formica-topped bed lockers on Male Chest, I was washed out in the repeated press of so many bodies. I could no longer believe in the talk around the commissioning table, or that words in newspapers or images on screen meant very much. Or changed the world enough to make a difference.

When it was over I was surprised to still be alive. Lucky.

SILENCES

Death comes in many guises. Whether we rage against the dying of the light or eagerly embrace the darkness, we must all find our own way. We shall all, man, woman, adult or child, answer to the mystery of our lives – our becoming – in our death. The person who we are, the deeds by which we defined ourselves throughout our days, will be the answer to our quest. And we shall encounter death in the lives of those we have loved, those we have hated and those we have casually known. On death's shore there will be no right or wrong, only a better or worse way to die. And there will be a lesson, too, in how to live, and how to love.

Whispering about death in Anglo-Saxon land – putting our hands over our ears, blinding ourselves with the Western Death Machine and going on pretending – doesn't change the mortal landscape. It just leaves you naked and exposed.

You will have to run that marathon alone.

When death comes for you out of a blue sky or at 2.34 p.m. on a grey day in the office, it can hit like a freight train right through your heart. Smashing your world into so many pieces that everything you ever did, everything you ever wanted, is right now so absurd, ridiculous, pointless, that there's no real reason why you don't step off the balcony, jump in the sea or walk right out into the traffic. Because what difference would it really make?

And although no one ever told you before, it's true: the sun can rise in the west. The floor can open up without warning. Walls split, empires fall, planes crash into buildings and lightning can strike from cloudless sky. With one shot the Celestial Sniper can destroy your life and leave you just an empty shell of a body to walk around with.

And death is so real that you can feel it, taste it, in every cell of your body.

The days and nights engulfed when you go washing-machine crazy, not sleeping, tumbling over and over in your mind as if somehow it, this thing, this how-you-hate-to-even-think-the-word thing, could be stopped, reversed. Erased.

The moment when you look down from the ceiling and see yourself answering the call that changed everything. Seeing yourself starring in the opening scene of what will be your own personal death movie, except it is not a movie and there is no happy ending.

*

Or the day when you discover a real secret. That when someone you know dies, even someone you love, there is nothing you can do to kiss it better. You can't replace the part, take it to the garage, write out a bigger cheque, find another doctor or make him, your dead husband, start breathing again.

The knock on the door too late at night. Uniformed strangers enacting some protocol, checking this is the right address for your sister and the sound of what they then say, 'accident', 'hospital', 'dead', ripping into the universe.

The day in the hospital – and the tests. Catching that piteous glimmer in the medic's eye. Knowing then there is no escape now from being always here on the ever-wrong side of the desk. The soon-to-be-the-dead-you side. The role iron cast. Wishing at that moment it was someone else. A stranger passing in the street. Quickly switching places so no one notices. Or cares – an alcoholic or a drug addict. An older person. The new-found victim sitting in this cursed seat doing the dying instead of you. Since they have nothing really to live for.

And it is just so wrong.

Hating them all.

Someone should know this shouldn't be happening or have happened.

Or you should have been warned. Ate some other diet. Or the doctors are confused. A mixed-up chart. Because you really, really don't want this to be true.

The moment you wonder how you ended up here in this shabby hospital box room with a pack of industrial tissues pre-prepared on the coffee table, waiting to hear the prognosis on your eight-year-old. Even though this was never meant to be in your life script. And no one ever said it would or could at home, at school or college. Or personally gave you a box of instructions or a party plan for dead daughters. Or said they kept them in stock.

Just like no movie showed you how to breathe right now when your chest is bursting. The panic flowing to your head. Because your precious innocent little darling, who never hurt a soul, doesn't deserve this. And you have never been so alone. So alone that it feels like the doctor is slitting you open with a hot branding iron right here now; your guts falling like steaming bloody meat to the floor. And it would feel better if they actually did cut you because it would make more sense than this overturned horizon where on the surface, the room, the people all remain the same as if the world was not so utterly changed and not so fucking cruel.

Or how cold, cold like a fridge cold. Cold like a stone lying outside on the ground cold. So cold you can see your breath in the air cold. Not warm like a human warm. But still so perfectly shaped like your wife, your dead wife feels on your lips when you kiss her forehead as she lies in the white coffin. The one you picked out for her, like a dress, in the red-tiled funeral home in that old mall off the highway, with its veneered teak waiting room and the stewed coffee machine, that so reminds you of that cheap motel where you first slept together. And you have to rush to the bathroom because you can't stop yourself weeping.

Middle-aged and alone, long after the funeral crowd have left. Standing next to the kitchen table, looking at the clock. Staring out through the kitchen window at the end of the garden disappearing in the dark; the grass is too long and the fallen leaves need to be raked away. Another thing on the to-do list. Wondering why your dead husband is so late because he really should be here for dinner by now.

Traffic?

Then it bursts up through your guts. Bawling your eyes out again, because, because, he's never, ever coming back through that door again.

Six months gone and everything is fine. It's all okay. Adjusting. You're reading the bedtime story. Sam adds his regular line, 'Goodnight Mommie in the sky,' and falls asleep.

But downstairs, because of the day. Because there wasn't any cereal, because you forgot. And the traffic bad and you lost your temper after another toilet 'accident' on the way home. And there's no one to tell and no one to help. Just you to get on with it. Like an electric shock you're suddenly so angry that if you could you'd shake her. Your silent, unanswering dead wife: 'Why the fuck did you always have to drive so fast?'

The office. How you hate all these shallow, superficial idiots who blabber on about their kid's school. Their stupid jobs. Problems with their computer. Or the internet. Recycling half-remembered garbage off the talk shows. Or quoting God back at you. When what you'd really like to do is pick their fucking laptop up off the desk, smash it over their heads and just say it straight: 'He's dead, he's dead, and I hope you fucking die too.'

And even when they do try to say anything, it only makes it worse. Just one word can set you off. Tearing up. Crying in front of them, shameless. Everyone embarrassed for you, not really knowing what to say or do next.

Death just sounds like a whisper in the West because we close our eyes and put our hands over our ears to mask the sound of others' keening. But on the day death comes for you the sound in your ears will be louder than thunder.

FRAGMENTS

Away from the cloak of the Western Death Machine, the dead are everywhere visible, in famine, plague and war. On a cloudy morning in southern Sudan, I stood by the grave of a child, nine-month-old Ayp Mo, who had died of starvation in the night amidst an angry swarm of hungry people at a charity feeding centre, less than a mile away. A dead child of famine. In our Western luxury, in our glut of obesity, dying of hunger is inconceivable to us. Something we only ever see on our TV screens or read about in history books. But the biblical curse of famine is not so far in the past. On my father's island, at the epicentre of the great Irish famines of the 1840s, the memory still lingers. In my mother's village, Ballinasally, whole families starved to death along with an estimated third, 2,000, of the impoverished island population. Nearly two centuries later, the island's population is still a third of the pre-famine level, and the abandoned potato ridges of scores of starved villages can be seen on the hillsides. In other parts of the world, wrought by endless civil war and the absence of roads and supply, famine is never more than two bad harvests away.

Staying alive in a famine is not like queuing for bread. It is a fight for survival between the weak and the strong. For the hungry, the hope of food draws them from their villages, walking forty, eighty, one hundred miles to dangerously congregate together in a strange place – the Western charity's feeding centre. Many, walking the long distances through the tall grass without food, will weaken further on the journey or die on the road. Disease soars as the population forages for barely edible weeds or consumes rotten flesh. Dysentery, diarrhoea, sometimes cholera, is inevitable.

At the feeding centre, half the newly arrived population will already be sick, shitting everywhere. There are no huts, no latrines, no wells and no power. In the stifling heat, every local water supply swiftly becomes a source of further contagion. The infected air is filled with the buzz of a billion vivid green bottle flies – so many swarming you fear to open your mouth – that feed on faeces and spread disease.

Then the strong, masquerading as the helpers of the white foreigners or as the local militia or the government, band together to tax the food haul for themselves. What remains is then passed around for everyone else to fight over in an orderly fashion. The weakest, those who cannot force their way through in the press of human desperation, are pushed down and back. No one is weaker than a lone young mother and a starving child. Deprived of the sustenance of her malnourished

mother's non-existent milk, and sick, the child Ayp Mo
had lost this fight and perished in the night.

In the midst of a multitude of other mothers and
babies in a makeshift tent, Ayp's body, wrapped up in
a bundle of rags, lay neglected, abandoned like a piece
of lost property on the dusty earth floor. Ayp's mother,
Agap Mo, was fighting on for her own life, patiently
queuing in line for enough food to save herself.

Just eighteen, tall and winsome, Agap Mo returned
after dawn to bury her own first-born child. I followed
Agap as she carried Ayp away alone in her arms from
the feeding centre to a makeshift burial ground, an unmarked potter's field on the edge of the limitless bush.
Once there, Agap placed the bundle, her dead child,
down on the ground and began to dig in the earth with
her bare hands. The earth was soft. It had rained in
the night. After fifteen minutes the hole was two foot
deep. There was no song, no words or crying out, just
the sound of far off birds calling and a flat horizon of
green bush. Then Agap lined the bottom of the grave
with the last of her possessions – an empty World Food
Programme grain bag – and laid the child within. In
a moment of tenderness, she slipped the child's tiny
wire bracelet from Ayp's wizened wrist and tightened
a piece of cloth round the skeletal child like a shroud.
Then Agap brushed the earth back over the child,
leaving only a raised mound and the infant's bracelet
as mark. Behind her, beyond her, other small mounds

marked out other graves and a thin stream of families, the wretched of the earth, came bearing more dead. Then Agap turned away back towards the cauldron of the feeding centre and was soon lost in the mingling crowd. There was no more ceremony.

At the edge of the child's grave, I wanted to pray. I wanted to call out to a God, the assembled company, someone, in this field of desolation, that a child should not starve to death and what I was seeing was a terrible event. That this naked death, so new and so ancient, a primitive unmarked grave no more than a hole in the ground, was wrong. But there was no God there in those famine fields. Just myself, Agap Mo, and the surrounding graves. I was powerless. So I stood and said nothing.

On a crowded ward in a hospital on the shores of Lake Malawi in the middle of Africa, I watched a twenty-year-old girl, Eliza Mwase, die of AIDS in a ward where everyone else was dying of AIDS, in a hospital where every bed had someone dying of AIDS, in a land so ravaged by plague there was no seeming hope of salvation.

It was one in the morning and Eliza tried to pull herself up in her deathbed for a sip of water but was too weak. 'It hurts, it hurts,' she called out in Chewa, the local language, as her aunts, Jane and Patricia, pulled her into a sitting position. Tenderly, as if soothing a child, the women repeated her name, 'Eliza, Eliza,' as they lifted a cup to her lips. Under the greenish light of a fluorescent tube, Eliza's hands writhed involuntarily at her wrist as if seeking to escape their dying host. As she tried to sip the water, Eliza coughed and the water spilt over her chin and down her front. She struggled to clear her lungs, her eyes blazed black, and she slumped back, uncomprehending, with the pain.

In the humid tropical air, the smell of soap mingled with the scent of a high musky, sweetish human sweat. A night rain, a light shower, began to patter on the ward's corrugated tin roof, dampening the screeching buzz of cicadas coming through the open windows from the surrounding trees in the hospital grounds. Two paces from the foot of Eliza's bed, a six-month-old baby slept beside his mother on the concrete floor. Every inch of floor space was covered either with patients' beds or with their guardians, their helpers like Eliza's aunts, who tend to every non-medical need. The dying and living are crowded in here, meshed as one, so close that you cannot walk between them.

In the morning, the sun will rise and these sleeping bodies will rouse themselves awake but not Eliza, now just three hours from her death. The rain began to drum steady on the roof, the noise of splashing waters filling up the ward, falling earthward, bathing the living and dying in the river of its embrace. It is the last sound Eliza will ever hear.

Eliza was just a village child who had succumbed to the glitter of a faraway city, working as a bar girl, until one of her boyfriends passed on a virus, a snippet of genetic code, that someone else had passed on to him. In Malawi it was not very difficult to become infected with HIV, the human immunodeficiency virus. Ten per cent of the adult population was already infected. Every sexual encounter, even with your supposedly monogamous partner, carried an unquantifiable risk of a lethal infection because the virus's latency could be as long as ten years. Your partner's previous partner's previous partner might never have known they had become infected.

In a country as poor as Malawi, where the average income is less than US$500, statistics are mostly a guess, but this plague was a literal decimation – killing one in ten of the population. In Chewa, AIDS is known as *matantanda athu omwewa* – meaning 'this thing we all have in common'. At least a million Malawians, out of a wavering population of around 10 million, have died of AIDS in the last two decades. A further million are infected with HIV. So many Malawians died that the life expectancy of a Malawian man fell to fifty-four years, twenty-eight years fewer than a European male.

No one was immune. Half of the Malawian parliament, a number of senior politicians' children, doctors and teachers, drivers, prostitutes, their customers, virtually anyone sexually active, had become infected and died. Eliza was just another victim of being too poor to protect herself. Of having no means of getting medical treatment to fight a human retrovirus that had invaded her body and was destroying her immune system's T-helper cells. If you were HIV-positive and got ill in Malawi, a country that has no real health budget, you were going to die.

In the city, Eliza was not the only one in her family to get sick. The first was her mother, Frieda, who died at forty-two, and then her father, Thomas, at forty-nine. With no one left to care for her, Eliza came home to the red earth of her grandfather's village by the shores of Lake Malawi, a freshwater lake almost as wide as a sea. Not that the local town of Nkhotakota was much of a place to come back to. It was a place between places, a way station on the road to somewhere else; a petrol depot, a line of shops, market stalls selling grilled meat or Chinese household wares, another line of bars and brothels with names like AK Paradise Store or the Za-bwino Bar. Nkhotakota was a place people came from, not to. But Eliza had no choices left. This was her last sanctuary. In her village, outside town, Eliza grew sicker and sicker until she ended up in the local Nk-hotakota District Hospital, a charnel house of suffering that made my time in Male Chest seem luxurious.

To walk its concrete corridors was to enter a living circle of Hell, where patients, two to a bed, lay to-gether befouled in their own diarrhoea, and death was everywhere. The virus burst out in the suppurating leg ulcers of a Kaposi's sarcoma patient on the Female General Medical ward. The virus queued in the night inside the emaciated bodies of the skeletal men, lining up for their meds, who occupied Male TB. It rolled on in the weeping genital herpes sores of a torpid twenty-nine-year-old tobacco clerk lying prostrate in Male General. It gathered in the infections and rashes of the wasting infant children ward on Paediatrics. This plague lived too in the bodies of many of the nursing staff. There was no end to this long day of dying. And no hope of change.

On the morning of her death day, her aunts took Eliza back home, wrapped in a shroud, on the metal floor of the hospital ambulance. They laid Eliza out and had a wake. They decorated the mud-walled hut where she lay with bunches of blood-red bougainvillea blossoms in old coke bottles, and lit the space with a glowing paraffin lamp. In the plain pine box, Eliza seemed impossibly small, a girl child whose haunting beauty, an African Helen, wrung at the heart.

And then the next day, after a night of keening, songs and prayers, the villagers carried Eliza in her coffin down to the seashore graveyard on a river of hands held at hip height, a conga line that flowed seamlessly to her red earth grave. Eliza was one of many, the row of freshly turned earth, the settling mounds of other adjacent graves, stretching away towards the lapping waters of the lake where fishermen's boats bobbed in the swell. Between that earth and the water, there was no masking death. No Western Death Machine. This plague was all around us, even inside the living bodies present; everyone had a brother, a sister, a parent or a child who had died; many of the funeral crowd were themselves infected. Yet life went on because there was no other choice, no means of protest, and no way through the walls of poverty that imprisoned every-one. The Western drugs, the antiretrovirals of the rich First World used to treat HIV, were beyond all reach.

I was humbled to stand there amidst such over-whelming death-courage. In our Western fear, where even the sight of the very ordinary dead is deemed upsetting, we would surely have crumbled in terror at such infection sweeping through our ranks, sickening and killing without respite. A decimating plague that could not be confined to a few scapegoats to be easily blamed for bringing such wrath down on themselves by their behaviour. Like famine, plague is something we only ever read about in history books. In our Whisper Death World we believe, or are told, such a holocaust could never happen to us. But of course it could.

The Malawians are poor beyond our imagining, but they remained strangely defiant, robust, in this engulf-ing catastrophe. They were indifferently brave in facing their own imminent mortality. Stoic. Men and women, old and young, got on with the lives they had, edging forward, going to school, to work, having sex, getting married, bearing children, getting older, burying their dead with dignity and waiting on without choice, as the Trojans before them waited too, for a remorseless fate to strike or pass.

In the lancing sweat of a Gazan summer, in 54 degrees of heat, I climbed the stairs of a half-bombed building to view and smell the rotting body of a casualty of war, two-year-old Ayman Matar. The child, still pitifully dressed in his little boy's green shorts, had just been dragged from the rubble of his home, a crushed apartment destroyed by an Israeli F-16 warplane's bomb forty-eight hours before.

The Gazans are the dispossessed, driven from their villages in 1948 in what is now southern Israel. They are the vanquished, their lands seized by their conquerors, and whose fate in the past, like Troy, was to disappear from history. Except the Palestinians have not disappeared and they live on in their defeat, surrounded – air, sea and land – by their implacable enemy. The barren sands of Gaza, a strip of refugee camps turned makeshift city, and now one of the most densely populated places on earth, is their refuge, their exile and their prison.

This endless conflict between the conquered and their conquerors is still unresolved. The war smoulders, erupts – as the Palestinians rise up again against their dispossession – and then falters back down in irresolution and failure.

Ayman Matar was 'collateral damage', a calculated trade-off on the size of the bomb needed under the Israeli intelligence plan to kill a military leader of Hamas, the main Palestinian resistance group, in an adjacent building with an aerial strike. The 1,000-pound bomb was dead on target, and so was Ayman when the shock wave of the explosion rippled through the surrounding apartments' thin concrete walls like a soldier's boot on a sandcastle. Six other members of Ayman's immediate family – his mother, three sisters, a brother – were killed, along with the Hamas leader and his family. Five other civilians also died. The youngest victim was Ayman's infant sister, Dina, who was twelve months old. The Matars had no knowledge that the Hamas leader, Salah Shehade, was secretly living with his family in hiding beside them. But even if they did know there was no possible defence against an F-16 attack. One hundred and fifty other people were injured and dozens of other homes flattened. Rescue crews had been digging in the shattered ruins for two days to retrieve the dead before they uncovered Ayman.

I was called in from the street and urged to come and see the child's body, which lay at the top of three flights of stairs, amidst the rubble of shattered apartments. For the Palestinian rescuers, the discovery of the child's body was a grim prize and a chance to show the outside world, via a foreign reporter, the cruelty of their enemy. In the dust, bustle and heat, it was hard to immediately grasp what I was seeing. The immense force of the explosion had pulverised parts of the building, turning concrete back into a powder that thickly coated every surface. At first all I saw was a bundle of rags buried in grey dust lying on a stretcher half inside a demolished room. And then within the mound I recognised the colours as a small boy's dark-green shorts. Then I saw the shape of a body and the outline of bulging eyes. I was looking at a dead child submerged in grey powder as if his flesh was already stone.

Ayman's body was intact. He had probably been suffocated in the dust cloud rather than crushed when the ceilings and walls of his home came in on him. In the staggering heat, the smell of decomposition – sweetish, acrid, nauseous – was gagging. All around us, other bodies waited, too, to be dug from these ruins.

In the narrow street outside, a vengeful crowd, corralled like an animal, screamed in frenzy for revenge. I had wanted to hear that scream. Some part of me still thought I should never flinch away from these sights, the dead child, the putrefaction, the cruelty and futile loss.

But in Gaza I struggled to understand myself. Being at the site of a mass killing in war was a different face of death. You could reach into the rubble yourself and pick up fragments – photos, baby clothes, intimacies

– of lives freshly obliterated. You could see the sweat on the faces of the enraged crowd and understand the despair of their powerlessness. You could glimpse what it meant to be the vanquished, the defeated, the dispossessed of history, who suffer without hope of respite. The abandoned. Yet on the stair, before the child's body, I had felt ashamed, a ghoulish voyeur. Exposed. What could I offer in return for this death? A few words or paragraphs printed? Another eyewitness report in another newspaper on another dead child killed in a war that had lasted already sixty years, with thousands of other victims that no amount of newspaper words had ever altered? A child's death that changed nothing apart from the pain inflicted on those who had loved him.

Fragments, like broken vases, cannot be reconstituted and made whole, unscarred. And these fragments of death remained what they always were; other lives torn in wreckage, lethal jetsam and flotsam, broken in strange tides of famine, plague and war. Parts of a former thing – linked back to lost purpose and other lost lives. I asked more questions than most other reporters and usually got different answers because I always had another purpose of my own, beyond the news story and the TV clip. I cannot now disown my death hunting. By being a chronicler of a kind, I think I became a wiser person. I saw more of the world than I expected and I learned how easily we can unravel civilisation in largely futile violence. But I failed to find the armour I wanted against death.

In Sudan and Gaza, and other places, you could see power and fear and our very human capacity to blind ourselves to wrong. You could catch a glimmer of the present unfold into history, measured most cruelly in the toll taken of other people's lives and the crushing of hope. In the West, we believe we are beyond the blood lust of Achilles and the savagery, and death of men, at the gates of Troy. Although it never mattered very much, I rediscovered for myself the opposite truth. Life can still be as easily taken, the slaughter of prisoners or the slaughter of civilians, as it was in the *Iliad*.

On the plane back, high above, safe in the sky, I realised, too, that the fragments of things that I saw and experienced could never teach me how to live with death in my own ordinary life.

LANDSCAPES

I finally gave up on death back in Ireland, standing by a grave in Dublin's Glasnevin Cemetery, watching a six-year-old boy weep uncontrollably for his father going down into the earth in a brown box. Ireland's Troubles were winding down in exhaustion and the war was almost over. By then, I had grown weary of reporting purposeless killings and weary, too, of trudging for miles on grey Ulster mornings behind the funeral cortege of another failed would-be murderer who had fumbled into disaster with his own bomb. I was sick of myself standing in the same picture, watching teenage boys intone supposed sacred texts, hymns of further blood and sacrifice, at the graveside as if thirty years of futile murder was not enough.

Glasnevin, with its legions of ordinary dead Dubliners, over a million graves, and stone forests of nineteenth-century headstones, is infamous as the last resting place for generations of IRA men who lost their lives – often killing each other – in the violent pursuit of the republican dream of a United Ireland. The grave-yard has a dedicated section, a place apart, a sacred pantheon, for the dead gunmen – the Republican Plot.

I was there for the funeral of one of the last of these fallen, another so-called martyr, who was shot dead by an Irish policeman in a bungled raid on a security van. The robbery was to raise money for guns for a new terrorist faction, a splinter group, who wanted to carry on killing and bombing after everyone else had tired and stopped. The dead man, who never had much in life, wanted glory and had now found it in his tomb. He was twenty-seven years old and left three children behind, with a fourth on the way. In dying for a hopeless cause he won a place – albeit shared with an older IRA man from the 1960s – in hallowed ground.

No amount of pageantry could mask the awkward symmetry, the grey burdensome weight of this day. Crowded around the coffin was a ragged mob of mourners, drawn faces on flabby bodies ruined by too many fags, drugs and poverty; their clothes, worn suits, denim jackets, football shirts, bearing the shabbiness of the urban defeated. A rearguard of the dispossessed.

Being Irish, before the funeral, the gunman's family had held a traditional wake which the organisation's leaders used to show off their new martyr. In a house on a grubby Dublin council estate, paint peeling off the walls, the gunman's corpse and open coffin were adorned with the symbols of the secret organisation he had died for. A black beret and black leather gloves, newly bought, had been placed on his chest to denote his membership of this so-called new republican army. Incongruously, next to the beret, stood a card, written in childish handwriting on the inside of a cornflake packet, from his six-year-old son. On the front of the card three capital letters were coloured in, 'I-R-A', and underneath in a scrawl, 'Bye, Bye Daddy'.

The squalor of the surrounding inner-city estate, the rubble-strewn streets, the graffiti and smashed cars, the sheer misery of a heroin-ravaged township, only added to a sense of hopelessness.

At the grave at Glasnevin, there was a grand-sounding funeral oration; praise for the fallen far-sighted hero, a call to arms, an oath of revenge, a pledge of allegiance to a future mythic republic that would never be. This death, the speaker said, was not an ending but a glorious new beginning in the armed struggle, a renewal of the long war, a blood annunciation. I knew their words already as I had heard the same speech, by now, many times before. The speaker stopped.

After a hesitant pause, as if even the organisers were unsure what to do next, a rotund bugler, belly bulging, incongruously played the 'Last Post' – a British army lament for their fallen dead – out of tune. Then there was another rite, the folding stiffly of the Irish tricolour flag that had been draped on the dead man's coffin. The flag was then solemnly passed to the child, as if the fabric itself could be a substitute for a father.

The child never stopped weeping, his tears running without shame down his cheeks. As we stumbled on through these hollow ceremonials, his sobs filled every moment of silence; unceasing, shameless, wailing like a keen, carrying his grief through the gaps in the gathered crowd up into the air and beyond into the fields of infinite dead around us. I too felt alone in the midst of the sullen, seemingly mesmerised crowd. I was nauseous, heart-sickened, at the emptiness in my own life. As the child wept on, all I saw around me was atavistic stupidity and abject folly. In that crushing pathos, I silently spoke out in my mind to the dead man:

I am a stranger here but I am the only one who will utter the truth though many others will also secretly share these thoughts. You're cold in the grave and we, your enemies and friends, will soon be nipping back to the pub for your funeral feast. We'll be safe inside, not left behind here in the dark ground, when the cemetery gates are locked tonight. Soon we will all be going for that comforting steaming-off-the-urinal-coming-out-of-the-chilled-graveyard-full-bladder-emptying warm piss. Your 'friends' and 'comrades' will, a few minutes later, be at the bar ordering drinks, talking about the day, the weather, themselves, the living, their politics. They will be warming up, washing away the memory of the day, and you, with pints of Guinness and ham sandwiches. After a few more pints, they'll all be going home; touching their women, their men, feeling the heat of their warm bodies, kissing their children goodnight, sleeping in a soft bed, maybe

making love. Getting ready for their tomorrows, school, jobs,
whatever. Forgetting about you and this empty dream for
which you supposedly died. You will be disappearing into
the limitless dead around us. No longer even a 'you' but a
phantasm, a fading locus of memory, dissolving away into
the strips of green grass, the gravel paths, the acres and acres
of stone monuments of centuries of dead Dubliners, the un-
remembered past, and these other forgotten lives that no one
cares about. Everyone, apart from the boy, is so very glad it's
you and not them; a lump of dead meat rotting in the box
in the earth. You died for nothing, nothing, to become just
another ghost in Hades.

I had thought my long quest in the land of the dead
would help me discover more about what it meant to
be human, to be mortal. I had searched through dozens
and dozens of destroyed lives for a shield to protect me
from the wound of sudden death. I had wanted something that would guide me as to how I should live my
life. But at that graveside in Glasnevin, in the abysmal
pity of a child's tears, I finally saw that all my death-
hunting had led me into a wilderness. The taste of
death in my mouth no longer renewed me; it just made
me more afraid. Death had lost all purpose. And so
had I.

VIGILS

The word when it came was simple – come Home. Sonny had lapsed into unconsciousness, the vigil begun, and death close. I caught a flight west and drove further west still into the endless luminescence of the island's summer solstice. A few miles off, a bright fog, a blinding white miasma, engulfed the adjoining mainland and the whole island in summer sea mist. Towns and villages slipped by barely glimpsed. Oncoming cars, houses, gorse hedgerows, sheep by the side of the road, emerged and disappeared again within seconds. With a cloak over the sun, the temperature dropped. All landmarks were lost, and it was easy to believe the long familiar road itself had changed and the lines between sand, rock and ocean blurred. That this unknown track would lead on to some other destination. Or straight into the sea. A great carpet of silence descended on the earth. There was no birdsong, no wind or wave, no rustle in leaf, no sight or sound of any other creature, donkey, cow, man or beast, in the blinding curfew.

Beyond the windscreen it was neither night nor day. An opaque brightness stole into the sky around four in the morning and hung there somewhere above us well past the following midnight. The ocean, the very sound of the surf, stilled and disappeared. Sheep, fence posts, the ruins of the old village, emerged and then receded again as the light faded or the mist thickened. In Dookinella, we lost the shadows of all things.

Inside the house, Sonny scalded the eye; bones and skin tight on the oversized skull, the bruised flesh flaring in jaundiced discoloration. The muscles in Sonny's neck had withered into nothing and his trunk and head jutted at an odd angle as if, without the support of the surrounding pillows, they would break apart in skeletal pieces. Known as *cachexia*, his body, in these end stages of his pancreatic cancer, had already consumed all muscle and fat to feed the brain. Earlier in the week, Sonny, on heavy sedatives, had drifted in and out of consciousness, gabbling about taking bets in a bookie shop. None of it made sense. Sonny was never a gambler. And then he fell into coma and lost all involuntary movement. His blue eyes locked open and filmed over. He could no longer swallow, blink or see. His lips were soon pitted with small brown scabs and the open mouth caught in a parched red circle that reached inwardly to the raw back of his throat. He panted in a huffy, shallow frenzy rather than breathed; each intake maniacally following on from its predecessor as fast as his skeletal ribcage could rise. His heart muscle, like a lone marathon runner left behind, was frantically trying and failing to clear the near toxic levels of CO_2

in his bloodstream. Sonny's body was blindly running on towards final collapse.

To the side of the bed, a catheter drained dark, forbidding urine. Behind Sonny's head to the right, stationed beneath the picture of Christ Our Saviour, an intravenous drip and morphine pump intermittently dripped painkiller into his collapsing veins. Our shepherd neighbour, Mikey Dan, dressed in his oilskins ready for the fields and sheep, came in early one morning to see his old friend and harshly voiced out loud what was thought but unspoken.

'What a terrible sight to see. That man would be better off dead.'

And then Mikey tenderly reached out to stroke the back of Sonny's hand.

In these death throes, Sonny was surrounded by life. The vigil ran night and day. There was always a someone – a daughter, a son, a sister, a relative, a neighbour – to watch over him from a bedside chair in the spartan bedroom. In their comings and goings, the chains of watchers never broke, sharing time together and time together again with Sonny. Watching and waiting.

Beyond the door of the dying room, the house was as full as at a wedding feast. Cars came and went hourly, disgorging payloads of visitors. Errands for fresh supplies were run. Tea and ham and tomato sandwiches were made and consumed and dishes washed by ever-changing shifts of neighbouring women in a kitchen-turned-cafeteria. Rough rotas for those keeping the vigil at Sonny's bedside were calculated, and the long watches into the night planned. Beds were shared and sofas commandeered for sleeping. Five of Sonny's six living children came home for his last days, one from California, and the sixth, and last, would be there for his funeral. Children and grandchildren, three, five and nine, tumbled under feet and wandered in and out of the dying room as the needs of the living and the dying fused together. So many mourners gathered for this living wake we had to be farmed off to further relatives and makeshift beds found for sleep.

I took my turn in the watch after midnight, to relieve my exhausted sisters as the house grew stiller. Father and son. Swapping roles. Now I was worried for him. Worried that Sonny was dying in pain, trapped and unable to communicate. After Bernard died, I asked Sonny what it was like to see your son die. His answer was spare and, for me at the time, unsatisfactory.

'I knew Bernard would die that day. I had seen it before on the island in both the strong and the weak. Great big men who you could never believe anything could happen to – now lying flat on their backs in the bed struggling. The heavy breathing, the exhaustion. I knew Bernard would not survive and I was worried for your mother. I knew your mother would take the death of Bernard hard. He had always been special to her, the only child she had ever breastfed. I wanted to help her in any way I could. I had to be there for her.'

Your dying son or your grieving wife? Who should you worry for? For Sonny the choice had been clear; accept what is beyond your power to change and look to the living.

Now, as his son, I wanted Sonny to die, his end to be, and pressed the button on his morphine pump to release more of the drug into his bloodstream to help make sure. The morphine should have eased any pain, suppressed his breathing and brought death closer. For much of the night I held his left hand to feel his pulse. The flesh was hot, dry, but the arm was limp, resistance less. The extra morphine brought no difference. Sonny, my father, was too far away from me already. In the middle of the night, along with my sisters, we turned Sonny in the bed to help relieve pressure and prevent bed sores. Beneath the sheets Sonny was even more of a mangle of bones, all angular shoulders and ribs poking out through the wizened skin. A piteous wreck. We fluffed the pillows around him, changed the sheets and laid him down in his death bed.

Morning came around four, and the world outside the window of Sonny's room grew slowly light again. The fronds of the front garden pampas grass, dripping with perspiration, appeared again through the mist. Beyond the further unseen front wall, the heavy engine of a tractor passed towards the shore for a purpose unknown. Another day was beginning even as our lives lost their boundaries, sleep-deprived, light-headed, nodding off and jolting awake, enshrouded in motionlessness, neither moving forward nor standing still. Just waiting for the end act – his death.

More visitors came and went. The full weight of Sonny's dying, these agonal sights, were neither hidden nor disguised from all who visited the household on this, the longest and last day of Sonny's life. The traffic to the house slowed mid-morning for Sunday Mass in the local church, and we found ourselves, Sonny's children, alone with our father in the house. It was a precious time, even within the wake. We gathered together round his bedside, softly shouting out our names as tears ran in a cascade down my sisters' faces and my own.

'I'm here Sonny. It's Teresa, Dad, and I love you . . .'

'I am here father and I love you . . .' the voices echoing in the tight room.

This calling out would be our final roll-call, a looping reversal, from the children he had once nursed and fed in the cot at the foot of his bed. And a small levelling of the debt we all owed him.

We moved now within a slower separation, measuring time in the hours till his death. Sonny will be dead by late morning, someone said. And then by noon. Or by tonight. A priest came in the late afternoon to deliver extreme unction to Sonny: a rite in the Catholic faith where holy oils are rubbed on the forehead of the dying close to their death. After gazing at Sonny for a few moments, the dog-collared priest, a well-fed Irish Friar Tuck, pronounced almost jocularly over his wasted journey.

'Och, there is a few hours left in him yet.'

The near contemptuous familiarity of his prediction, delivered like a farmer sizing up a cow in labour, stung like a blow to the face. How dare a priest, anyone, say such things? It felt callous. But as it turned out the priest was right. More troubling though was the priest's tone of voice, his confident off-hand lack of reverence, towards Sonny's imminent death. A mundane fearlessness. Death was an everyday event, another act in life, to be shared between the dying and the living.

Sonny never changed or gave any sign of mortal recognition. The frenetic machine of his body ignored the sacred oils of absolution, the calls and prayers of the living, the morphine jolts, the tears of his children, and battered on blind. Sonny, a biological ruin, had become the universal dying animal; the sweat-laden skull poking up through crocheted blankets, a deeply unconscious clattering bundle of bones and breath, spiralling forward towards certain end.

REMAINS

Sonny was dressed in his wedding suit when I saw him next.

He had a *marbh fháisc*, a death binding, wrapped round his head to keep his jaw shut as if, overnight, he had been caught fighting in a rugby brawl. His eyes were closed, their lids weighed down with the old jet black Victorian penny coins, and in between his bloodless, knitted fingers was a trail of rosary beads. He was wearing the same dark brown suit that he had worn fifty years before.

Sonny had died just before dawn's first light. I wasn't with him. As that day's vigil bled away into night, I had gone for sleep in a nearby house. Taking over, my sister Angela and brother Martin had been changing the sheets in the bed after Sonny's catheter leaked. When they turned him on his side he gave a small start and then stopped breathing. Sonny's children waited together a few moments and then called out for the rest of the household. More decades of the rosary were sung, our *bean chaointe* keening the opening verses, and more watchers returning the chant through their tears. This agony was over.

Sonny's heart had stopped but his death had only just begun. Sonny's body would be with us amidst his children, his clan, his people, till the grave. No one called for an ambulance, an undertaker or the authorities to help; Sonny was already home with us. After the sounds of the last rosary were said, and their tears dried, Teresa cleared the room. Under the guidance of my Aunt Tilda, she began to wash Sonny's body in much the same way the Trojan women washed Hector's. Using a basin and face towels, both women cleansed Sonny from head to foot, packing the orifices with cotton wool to prevent the seepage of fluids. The two women washed, dried and combed his hair and gave Sonny his last ever shave. Then, after slowly dressing him in his suit, Tilda tied the *marbh fháisc* under his chin to keep the mouth closed and laid the old pennies as weights on the eyes to close them. Before rigor mortis set in, they knitted Sonny's now bloodless, yellowed fingers together across his chest and threaded a rosary between. Sonny, as he knew he would be, was being prepared for his next audience in his coffin at his wake in the adjacent sitting room. And word of his death was already spreading through the villages, even though it just after six in the morning.

I walked into the house and went straight in to see him. Alone with my father, I spent a few minutes in the bare room holding his clasped hands, touching his hair. The blood had drained from his face and hands, rendering them pale. I kissed him on the forehead. When the dead cool, their flesh feels like ice cubes in a rubber glove, but Sonny was still warm and soft. I was truly happy for my dead father and for this heart's comforting. This death, so different from Bernard's in a hospital cubicle, was a blessing. I had no tears; this course had ended as we all knew, and he knew, it would.

No matter how many dead bodies you have seen before, the sight of our personal dead is an existential wonder. Sonny's body, his remains, were in that utterly exact word – lifeless. A baffling facsimile of someone you knew intimately, who now lies before you like a stopped engine, without animating current. I had no need of memory. Sonny's corpse was a visible, tactile, irrefutable statement of his present and eternal deadness, and my own fatherless future.

Around Sonny's cooling body the house was a frenetic hive of preparation. All the paraphernalia of sickness; the pills, the morphine pump, the special mattress designed to prevent bed sores, had already been packed away. The women of the house, Angela, Teresa, cousins, were hoovering, dusting and moving ornaments in a frenzy of spring cleaning at seven in the morning. At other wakes, it is not uncommon for the smell of freshly repainted walls to linger in the air. Furniture was being shifted and chairs rearranged. An empty space, coffin shaped, was marked out in the sitting room, along the back wall on the right-hand side of the room. A small table with tapers and candles, was placed where Sonny's head would lie, just as the ancient Greeks and Romans did with their dead.

In the midst of sofas being moved, Teresa showed me a small white envelope.

'Did you still want a lock of his hair?'

Sometime in the blurry days of the death vigil I had asked for a lock of Sonny's hair, a token of my father, and during the laying out Teresa had remembered. I could not hold on to my sick and dying father in the narrow room becoming death, but Sonny's hair was still strong and luscious, even as his body decayed. The silvery grey lock was a link to a chain of memories of the living father I knew; tilting his head forward to the left at the car mirror, frantically combing the bouncy, unruly wave, a last minute of grooming, before we visited relatives. Or combing the dust out after a week's work together, father and son, on a building site. In the intimacy of those shared days, I had watched Sonny comb his hair that way a thousand times 'Yes, I do.'

Teresa handed me the envelope. Inside was a steely grey-white lock. I have it still.

Outside, a slight breeze got up and the haze of the last few days finally lifted. The immense horizon of sky and ocean, the waves, the two mountains Minaun and

Croaghaun, came back to us in a dull white light as if the engine of the world was restarting and the next act about to begin.

On the island a lot of people come to wakes, and they need somewhere to sit alongside the dead. Someone phoned the landlady of a nearby bar to borrow bar stools, and I drove over with my younger cousin Stephen to collect them. The landlady opened up for us, and we gathered a pile of stools together and put them in the car. From somewhere, Stephen suggested we have a pint of Guinness. It was eight in the morning and, like most people, I don't drink beer for breakfast. But on Sonny's death day a pint of Guinness in an empty Irish bar just seemed like the most natural thing in the world. It was a strange moment. Ageless. Time had stopped. We were enfolded within the wake, the onward press of events already predetermined. I felt absolved of any responsibilities as if I was being carried along by a tidal current.

'Yeh, let's have a pint. It's not every day that your dad dies.'

'Good man.'

The landlady slowly poured two pints, let them settle, and then topped them up, carving out two shamrocks in the foamy head. I leant in and took a swig. The pint was creamy, and from the bar's front window you can look out at the Atlantic breakers batter away at the jagged reaches of the Minaun cliffs pretty much as they have battered away forever.

Sonny died young. The previous spring he had been on the bog, bending down below the knee, cutting deep into the sodden bank with a two-sided spade, called a *slain*, and throwing out heavy, wet, ten-pound peat turfs to dry in the wind. Cutting turf, the main source of winter fuel on the island, is hard physical work, taxing the strongest of bodies. Sonny, on the threshold of seventy, but still immensely strong, could work away for hours seemingly unbothered by the ardour of the task. Whether he was shovelling muck or sawing wood, Sonny always had a grace and skill to the way he handled tools. In my clumsiness, I still envy his deftness in the labour of men. He was never in doubt of purpose or seemingly wasteful of energy.

My father could so easily have had another ten or fifteen years hammering away at his works, digging his garden and going shoring every morning with Darcy. We only have this mortal world and Sonny was not Lucky. I regret his early loss.

Sonny though would have dismissed the thought. Under the sun, death comes when it comes. There is no court of appeal for the mortal; no logic, right or wrong; only a place, a time and the readiness.

Our weakness with death in the West stems from

our very denial. Death is most often seen as tragic happenstance, a usurping by a surprise enemy, a conspiracy against our limitless possibility; a singular meteor falling from the heavens, not a common rain shower. Away from the quiet oblivion of the old folks' home, we rail against cancer, disease and cellular mitosis. We run charity events and fundraising campaigns to challenge this terrible thing from ever happening again. We adorn our lapels with coloured ribbons and our wrists with armbands, though oddly we never visit the dying, go see the dead or attend their funerals. And death is something we still never, ever want to talk about.

On the island, no one writes about death, but they do go to funerals and talk about the dead and visit the dying, all the time. Death is an everyday occurrence, nothing special, and it is this scale by which any dying is judged. Sonny's time had come and whatever could have been and never was, or should have been and wasn't, in this ordinary man's existence was over. The mystery of Sonny's life was laid out in his freshly cooling corpse, in the actions of his life as it was lived not dreamed, in the works of his once dirt-encrusted hands, and our memories of his fathering. Sonny's life as son, husband and father had at least been a full measure, a life lived. Sonny's coming wake could be sad but it would never be tragic.

★

Stephen and I sipped our pints and sat and watched the long Atlantic breakers come through the bay to shore, wave after wave, thousands of miles in the making, ploughing the great green ocean, expending themselves in flurries of white spray against the cliffs of Minaun. When our glasses were empty we drove away into the soft morning stillness of the coming day.

On the way back to Dookinella, I stopped off at a ruined Franciscan monastery and gathered flowers for the house. The island's rhododendron season, when hedgerows on the road burst out in a mass of its purple flowers, was just finishing. The monks had come to the island in the 1850s and fought and died in the trenches of the old religious war that raged for half a century. Back then, their monastery on such a remote island must have been a forbidding posting – primitive, cut off, bleak. A life devoid of easy comforts or many prospects for an ambitious young man; an outpost on a far frontier, with no path or hope of return to Rome or glory. Over the following century the monks built up their small monastery, adding a bell tower, a beautifully illuminated chapel, farms and school rooms, and taught generations of island schoolchildren. By the 1970s, the religious war long forgotten, their brotherhood dwindled, collapsed, and the monks retreated, abandoning the monastery and the island. The work of generations, every hard-won endeavour, fell into decay. Broken open to the wind, the monastery's chapel ended up shamefully as a makeshift sheep and donkey pen; the monks' ornate, hand-painted frescos, countless hours of devotion to their God, crumbling off the walls into the shit and manure on the floor. Utter ruin. Sadly and sweetly all that remains of the spent promise of their lives is their old enclosed apple orchard, which still blossoms and blooms with fruit each year long after they have perished.

Not that the monks themselves are far away. Just a few feet from the broken chapel lies their bare graveyard. The entrance is adorned with a stark devotional Franciscan marker whose words date from a thirteenth-century poem: 'Welcome Sister Death'. For over a hundred years, every Franciscan brother slept, ate, drank and died within yards of the same graveyard where, like his predecessors, he knew he would be buried. What if those monks knew what was to become of their lives' work? Would they think the sacrifice, the denial, the absence of the comfort of women, their sterile brotherhood, worth the cost? Or would they turn back?

There is no answer. Time moves in one direction and we are without the power to unmake our chosen fate. Who are we, in our generation, to judge the monks' strength to live so openly in death's embrace, when we shun any mention of our own? The finest flowers of all can, and most often do, bloom unseen by a wider world. Will our own ordinary lives in time bear more value, legacy or worth than these dead monks of a fallen religious empire?

On Sonny's death day, most of the rest of the island's rhododendron flowers were gone, the soft purple leaves rotting brown. But in the trees the monks planted, some now over one hundred feet tall, there was ideal shelter for the late flowers of summer and a few bright tyrian purple blossoms sparkled. I gathered them in my arms, breaking off the woody stems by hand; the very last beauty of another generation. A gift from the dead for my father's wake.

BURDENS

At eleven in the morning, I went coffin shopping with my sisters and brother. We drove over to Ted Lavelle's, who ran a bar, a petrol station, hired out lawnmowers and marriage cars, and did a bit of undertaking on the side. Ted was famous, or infamous, on the island for being the first undertaker to open a funeral parlour in an industrial shed on his garage forecourt. Behind a brown hardboard door, next to the garage shop and off to the side of the petrol pumps, the deceased could now lie in state in an open coffin for a few hours rather than in their own home. The Western Death Machine was here on the island, too, and the rite of the wake fading.

At the funeral parlour, mourners would come, shake hands with the bereaved, offer condolences and pray over the deceased. There were chairs on which to sit and chat but nothing else. Most mourners came and left within the hour. After a few hours' visitation, the dead were taken to church. Ted's parlour was an option some families now chose for convenience or to limit the time given over to elderly relatives who had died in nursing homes or in hospital. Death on the island was beginning to be veiled, diminished and slowly 'professionalised'. Some of the daily death notices on the radio now came with warnings: 'House strictly private.'

Sonny, in contrast, would be 'reposing in his residence' in the sitting room and would be with us, night and day, until his coffin left for the church. Our visit to Ted had another purpose. There are no professional pallbearers on the island. The carrying of the dead, into and from the church altar and onto the grave, rests on the shoulders of their kin, hopefully their sons. To be carried by those of your own house to your grave is an ancient tribal blessing – a life and death hope, that you will multiply and prosper, bear children, die amidst your family, your community, and still be loved at the end of days.

To carry the weight of your own dead, to link arm to shoulder with your brother pall bearer, whoever that might be, shuffling forward in three sets of pairs, in sight of the congregation, is another communal rite of the wake, another fusion of the individual within the wider community. An honour. For those chosen, the wedge of the coffin on neck and shoulder bone is both a physical and symbolic act of manhood that binds again the dead, the living and the dead-to-be; just as we together carry our father/mother/sister/brother today, then so too will we in turn be carried one day by our brothers, our sons, our kin. When grandfather Pat Toolis died, he too had wanted his coffin to be carried by his own male line, his sons and grandsons. Our clan is so small – there were never that many Toolis males to go around – so Sonny asked me and my elder brother Francis to come home especially to fulfil that wish. And we did.

With Sonny, my sisters wanted to try and take on the burden and honour of carrying his coffin. It is unusual for women to act as pall bearers, so our visit to Ted's had another purpose; to test out the coffin for weight. Upstairs in his bare storeroom, amidst the petrol-driven lawnmowers, Ted laid out the various options of his still plastic shrink-wrapped coffin inventory. We could go for a solid plain oak at £700? Or the lighter pine inlaid with elaborate reliefs of the Last Supper with Jesus and his disciples and plastic gilt handles at £400? And then there was the mahogany with a tufted cream satin interior finish. We tried the pine, then the oak, carrying the empty coffin on our shoulders – two brothers, two sisters, back and forth across the long expanse of the store room. The oak felt a bit on the heavy side, the mahogany heavier still. We settled for the pine, and the £400, and after a bit more shopping for bread, ham, tomatoes, drove back to Dookinella in preparation for the wake. Ted followed behind alone, within the hour, with our newly bought coffin in his hearse.

At the house he parked just outside the garden gate and asked for a hand. Like moving a stray piece of furniture, I helped Ted carry the empty coffin up the front path and into the sitting room, manoeuvring back and forth, to make the ninety-degree turn into the small bedroom where Sonny lay. Ted placed the coffin on the bed beside Sonny and opened the lid. Instructing me to hold Sonny's feet, together we reached over and lifted Sonny up from the bed and into his coffin. It was easy; Sonny had shrunk in his illness and probably now weighed no more than six stone. Ted felt Sonny to check if rigor mortis had set in. It had. He and Teresa then removed the *marbh fháisc* and the heavy pennies. In the sitting room, Ted lined up two triangular stands for the coffin in the allocated place. We swung the filled coffin out of the bedroom and into sitting room, gently placing it down on the stands in front of the rows of borrowed bar stools. Sonny, eyes and jaws closed and rosary finger kneaded, was ready for his audience.

KEENING

Every death is different and every death the same, and a wake follows an ancient pattern where our oldest identities, female and male, determine the roles. Not long after his corpse was laid out in the sitting room, the first of Sonny's four sisters, my Aunt Kathleen, arrived. On seeing her dead brother, Kathleen burst into tears, calling out his name and reaching to touch and kiss him in the coffin. At the sight and sound of Kathleen's tears, a wave of emotion recaught the room and my sisters, and all the women, cried out in turn. I wept too. The unashamed emotion, their bodily embrace, was a keening, a raw wash, that rose, gripped the heart and gradually fell away.

After her own act of mourning, Aunt Kathleen sat down in one of the chairs close to the coffin, taking her place amongst the chorus, the *mná caointe,* the wailing women. Aunt Kathleen's mourning was the beginning of a rite where the core female relatives, daughters and sisters, surround the body of the dead and dominate the main stage of the wake. Kathleen was soon joined by Sonny's other sisters Mary and Margaret, my mother's sister Tilda, and my cousin Ellen from our childhood hay making days. Each mourner who entered the house would pass up the line of these women, shaking hands, hugging, offering soft words of comfort, before reaching and praying at Sonny's coffin and then touching or kissing his corpse.

A steady stream of villagers came through the front door: cousin Bernadette, heavily pregnant, and her young daughters; old sheep farmers in wellington boots and baggy tweed jackets; and our egg-selling neighbour, Nora, an elderly grandmother with a cane and floral headscarf declaiming over the close heat of this soft day, the loss of Sonny and how fine a man he looked in his coffin. There were other cousins whose connections in blood I never really understood and distant neighbours I had barely met. The house filled, emptied and filled again. Hands were shaken again, and again and condolences offered.

'Sorry for your trouble.'

This ritual of mourning repeated itself as it was supposed to until it dwindled into routine. The tempo of emotion rose and fell. If the new mourner was a close relative there would be a further collective crying out, a cathartic venting of grief, as they passed up the line of women. Each repetition draining away the reservoir of everyone's tears. There was no shame in this sorrow, no holding back, no stiffening of the lip.

Keening was once a profession. For thousands of years the Greeks, the Hindus, the Romans, the Jews, the

Celts, procured and paid wailing women to orchestrate lamentation at funerals. The last Irish professional *bean chaointe*, died in the 1950s, and the formal art of keening was lost until only the very old on the island still remember hearing the plaintive, bare cry in Irish. In Dookinella our *mná caointhe* were less formal, less ordered, but still turned back into the past for the physic comfort of crying, keening over the dead, around Sonny's coffin.

Nothing had changed in the wake. Gela Painter, a sixth-century BCE Athenian artist, painted the exact same scene on funerary terracotta panels 2,500 years ago: weeping women close to the corpse and the men at the back looking awkwardly on. The keeners at Sonny's side in the same ritual were reaching back beyond the weeping women of Jerusalem, back beyond Hector, and probably as far back as the Neolithic tombs on Slievemore mountain. Back further than we will ever know.

Unsure in my maleness, of my place in this feminine chorus at Sonny's wake, I looked on awkwardly, too. The tenderness and grief of the keening women was not just an act of mourning for Sonny but another ritual of passage, and of communal renewal. Through this chorus of women and their daughters there was the promise of new life to come, an overcoming of the wound of Sonny's death, a heart's healing. Children would be born, new lives created; the wombs of the many, fertile, giving, would transcend this loss. So like the male figures in ancient Greek pottery, I too hung back on the edges and watched.

After passing through the women and praying over Sonny in his coffin, each mourner would find a place amongst the borrowed bar stools to sit, chat and pass the time. We settled in for the long day and night ahead. A wake is a gathering, a social event, a chance to remember the dead but also gossip with the living over the price of sheep, the stock market, the weather or the division of the dead man's possessions. Nor was there any age bar. Sonny's grandchildren played with their toys at the foot of his coffin or wandered from room to room. Or else were captured and passed around from great-aunt to great-aunt for the comfort of cuddling toddler flesh. My nine-year-old nephew, Sean, dashing around for purposes unknown, would casually ruffle Sonny's hair every time he ran through the room on his way to play somewhere else. Teresa lifted her three-year-old son, Chris, up to coffin height so he could see and stroke the face of the grandfather he knew as 'Pappi'. Unperturbed, Sonny lay still dead in his coffin, but around him the room filled with a roar of conversation and laughter.

A wake too is a feast. Mourners must be fed, watered and nourished. Close female neighbours had taken over the kitchen and were feeding batches of wake-goers in consecutive sittings. Once one sitting was finished I would be despatched to the cramped sitting room to encourage the onward flow. There would always be a ritual refusal.

'Ah. No I won't.'

'Ah no do.'

'No, I won't.'

'Ah you must.'

'Okay, I will.'

A handful of conscripted mourners would then walk past Sonny's coffin and sit down to eat a few feet away in the kitchen. It was a traditional Irish summer feast; ham and tomato sandwiches, tea, malt loaf, mountains of biscuits and gallons of strong tea. Once these mourners were fed, they circulated back towards the wake room whilst others slipped away home.

As late as the 1950s, along with the coffin, a standard island funeral order would include a gross (144) of clay pipes and plug tobacco. At Sonny's wake, the snuff and clay pipes had fallen away, but, eager for a purpose, I continually circulated with a plate of cigarettes encouraging our mourning guests to take one and thus inadvertently shorten their lives a little further. As the evening wore on, I was tasked, too, with offering around rather warm bottles of Guinness, but only to the men. Rather than real drinking, it was more of a wetting of the lips. No mourner had more than two small bottles of beer the whole night. We had whiskey as well, but most of the mourners refused. I do remember offering glasses of sherry, but somehow it was not deemed appropriate for the women present to drink any alcohol at all.

Past wakes were far more boisterous gatherings and strong drink for the women, the *bean chaointe*, deemed a necessity. In 1689, an English traveller and bookseller John Dunton witnessed a wake and funeral in Galway.

Just before the corpse was taken out of the barn I saw about 20 women guzzling usquebagh or aqua vitae. I enquired who they were and was told they were the Mná Caointe, or the howling women, who had this given to them to support their spirits in that laborious work. And a horrid cry was immediately set up where some hundreds joined in concert. It was such as you cannot conceive nor I express, but such a peal it gave my ears as deprived them for some time of their hearing.

In the binding of the wake, mourners and the bereaved each have their parts to play, a checklist of mirrored rites and duties to be performed. It was important for each mourner to reach for my hand as the son of the dead man and offer their personal condolences.

Sorry for your trouble.
Sorry for your trouble.
Sorry for your trouble.
Sorry for your trouble.

My hand was wrung so many times, by so many distant kin, the bones began to ache. For the mourners, the handshaking was an obligation, a necessity to affirm their presence and share in this mortality. Sonny's death could not be glossed over just by turning up and being one of the crowd. His death had to be proclaimed time and time again in word and a gripping handshake. For the mourner touching the bereaved, like touching a corpse, is its own inoculation; we see and touch the channel of death before us but return back unscathed, renewed through the closeness of contact.

Sorry for your trouble.

At first this constant wringing embrace, the repeated cliché, felt like a tedious formulaic repetition. But somewhere in the number of the act, after dozens and dozens of handshakes, I felt the grace spread within the exchange.

Sorry for your trouble.

In the death of Sonny, what else could anyone offer? Their presence here was an act of mortal solidarity. The handshake and words were both a felt offering and an enforced exorcism. Again and again, bereaved son and mourner, we were saying out loud together that the world had changed, my father was gone and there was no going back. The wake was pulling all of us forward into acceptance of Sonny's deadness.

As they gripped my hand, many of the weathered, unfamiliar faces named a man I had never known. Old men, their skin cleaved by decades of labour in the sun, told of how in their generation they had known Sonny; their lives, like his, flowing back and forth into exile. They spoke of cities and worlds, journeys and times before I was born, remembering other dead I never knew.

'I knew your father through my brother Michael. He's gone now, too. We worked together on the potato squads in Scotland. Oh, it must be forty years or more now.'

Others had never left the island and remembered schooldays through the green fields and the chain of life that had bonded each to the other in this community.

'He was a fine piper, your father. We were in the Dookinella band together. I was a piper, too. I'll never forget your father teaching me how to play "Flowers of the Forest" for a St Patrick's Day.'

This rough accounting, a reassembling of many of the fragments of the past of a man, and a father, was a shock and a comfort. However much we think we know them, our parents' lives have their own mysteries. We judge them from below, not the side, capturing snapshots of the lives above us – a couple posing for the camera on their wedding day – never seeing the run of their lives before and beyond us.

As the evening wore on, the crowd thinned and changed. My older aunts slid away for sleep in readiness for the reassembly of the chorus tomorrow. Younger mothers, like my cousin Bernadette, took their children home for beans on toast, school homework, evening TV and the rest of their lives. The balance of the wake slowly shifted away from women to men.

As the light fell in Dookinella, another ancient assembly began to gather. Old bachelor farmers in brown suits from isolated cottages on the bog roads, with clipped accents so thick I could barely understand what they were saying, began to fill the front rows. Some still wore old-fashioned flat caps but others were bareheaded, dressed in loose jackets and ties, and spoke with a confident authority.

'You're Sonny's lad. I knew your father well. I remember being here in this house for his wedding, your mother and father. We had a barrel of beer.'

There were some younger men as well, mid-thirties. I recognised them from the road, driving tractors, or amidst the crowd in the local bar, but to whom I had never spoken. Somehow they all knew me but felt no need to introduce themselves by name as they reached out to shake my hand.

'Sorry for your trouble, Kevin.'

Perhaps they were there all the time. Although they had nothing to gain, this band of mortal brothers was another ritual of the wake, the male quorum, endured and inured, prepared to sit for the night on backless chairs and guard the passage out of a departed soul, just like they had done before the fall of Troy.

223

RITES

In the *Iliad*, the ghost of Patroclus, after being killed by Hector, appears in a dream to his lover Achilles and begs to be buried swiftly to bring an end to his torment of being refused entry to the gates of Hades. 'The ghosts, the phantoms of the dead are keeping me away, they will not let me cross the river to join their number and I am left wandering.'

Without proper funeral rites, the unquiet dead remained stranded, disordering the lives of the living, bringing chaos into the living world.

When the other great Homeric hero, Odysseus, enters Hades in *The Odyssey*, the first troubled soul he encounters is one of his own sailors, Elpenor, who died 'unwaked and unburied' on Circe's enchanted island. Elpenor pleads with his master for his ship to return to the island, recover his body and wake and bury him properly, and threatens the anger of the gods if Odysseus refuses. The duty to the dead, like Antigone's defiant reburial of her traitor brother Polynices in Thebes, transcends other loyalties.

Although we shun the bodies of our ordinary deceased, we too still share in these Homeric obligations to the dead. We believe a special class of the physical dead – the bodies of warriors – must be returned from their falling place on a battlefield thousands of miles away, back to their families to be buried with military honours in sacred ground. The armies of the West still strive to bring their battlefield dead away from foreign fields, sometimes decades after conflict ends, like the lost soldiers of the Vietnam War. Or pay ransom, as the Israelis have, for the return of their soldiers' remains. The Gazan father Diab Hamid, who wanted his Jewish enemy to return the scraps of his suicide bomber son Tariq, was acting on the same impulse – to bring his dead boy away from strangers to a final resting place. To bring him Home.

On the island, recovering the lost bodies of the dead, bringing them back for proper burial, remains an imperative obligation. When my godfather, Michael Cafferkey, and two of his shepherd companions were swept out to sea, hundreds of volunteers joined the hunt to find them. The search teams combed hundreds of miles of dangerous rocky coastlines, amongst the cry of gulls and deep sea swell, for nineteen days, until the men's bodies came Home from the ocean to be safely buried back with their ancestors on the slopes of Slievemore.

After an Irish Coastguard rescue helicopter crashed just north of the island, the sister of one of the two crewmen, whose bodies were lost at sea, appealed to fishermen to join in a co-ordinated search for the re-covery of their bodies. 'My parents need him Home, my sister-in-law needs him Home. My nieces need him Home. They have to come Home now.'

Even with the regular dead, this longing for safe burial at Home, after a lifetime of exile in America or England, is seen daily in the undertakers' hearses lined up to meet the inbound Ryanair flights at the local Knock airport. Beyond the cloak of the Western Death Machine, the bodies of the dead matter.

We have a deep and natural need for such proper endings. Closure. Dreaming of our dead is a common, almost universal, psychological reaction to grief. How could it be otherwise? That we would instead pack up our hearts, our longings, our love, overnight? Forget our flesh and blood and walk on alone in the darkness without them? After a time, for most of us, these apparitions fade and then cease, but for some the wound of loss never heals and the dead continue to haunt the world of the living. In Gaza and Israel, I always asked the family of a suicide bomber the 'dream question'.

'Do you ever see your dead son in your dreams?'

The answer was always yes. Most said their dead son or daughter spoke to them from a place that was green and lush, *a Jannah,* a paradise. In the burning slums of the West Bank and barren sands of Gaza, perhaps such dreams were a way of tending the wound, bearing the heartfelt loss and absolving their child and themselves of the stain of blood taken in the suicide blast.

You don't have to believe in Hades or Freud to understand how unresolved grief creates a mythology of a disturbed afterlife and how the torment of an unburied Patroclus heralds chaos for the living.

For our forebears, a wake and funeral were rites of closure that complete the ancestral life–death cycle, resolve grief and restore the natural order of the universe. Our ancestors believed that the dead needed the intervention of the living – prayers, food, spells – to help a departed soul make safe passage into the afterlife and find eternal rest. The dead had to be accompanied, waked, by living watchers as part of that journey through at least one solar cycle – day, night and then day – in the aftermath of their death. Hidden inside such a ritual is another ancient belief that somewhere in these hours of mingling darkness a portal opens between the living and supernatural worlds through which the soul of the deceased departs.

Believing that the restless dead have powers to unravel the world of the living also makes a wake a dangerous place. Anthropologists define wakes as liminal rites, a stage where the forces of life and death contend for dominance, a place of powerful magic. Our forebears were afraid that the portal was not just one way; when the passage to Hades opened hordes of the unquiet dead could cross back to invade the living world. The watchers, as old as the quorum that watched over Hector's body in Troy, are not just there to guard the soul of the departed out but also to man the Gates of Chaos against an insurgent tide, a satanic horde ready to crash through and destroy us all.

If you asked them of course the quorum would just say they're here to do the decent thing and show support for their neighbours. But in Dookinella these aged men, known as the 'stickers', were the lineage descendants of all those who have waked with the dead on the high slopes of Slievemore and both before and after the fall of Troy; living on in each other's death and dying in each other's lives; passing these rites and obligations between the living and the dead down through the generations. And as we passed through the long, still, uncomfortable hours of Sonny's waking they began quietly to speak of other lives and other dyings.

I was sitting in the row at the back, resting my shoulders against the wall, when I first overheard the speaker, a younger man, late thirties, talking to a small group of men in the line beside him. I heard one of the other men call him by name, Jack. I didn't know him, though maybe I had met him before. In the maze of common names and bloodlines on the island it can be hard to exactly pin down which Kilbane, O'Malley, Lavelle or Gallagher son you are talking to or talking about.

Jack was a cousin of someone or other; maybe he was a cousin of mine. He was dressed in a blue jumper and dark jacket and a pair of rugged boots. His face was weathered by sun and wind and he had the thick strong hands, nicked by cuts and wounds, of those, like Sonny, who work the fields. He had tousled black locks, long to his shoulders, and piercing blue eyes. Handsome. He was smoking, drawing the smoke deep into his lungs, holding centre stage, looking at his audience looking at him, as he spoke. The voice shone with a measured cleverness. There was something about him, the lilting accent, the easy drawl, the lustrous dark hair, the wildness of the look, the animated face, the straightforward masculinity, that drew you to him; he must have been a great pub storyteller.

'We were over in England working on a big house, finishing off doing the grounds. It was a huge place set in five or six acres in Essex. It was an old house, Georgian, but the family had done it up, built an extension, garages. The man had an office at the back as well. He was some kind of property developer, who worked in the Middle East. Saudi or somewhere like that. Very English. He was always flying away on business. He had a wife and two daughters. Rolling in cash; a Range Rover for her and a Jaguar for him in the driveway. A sitting room the size of this house. Huge. The mother-in-law was living with them as well. She said she'd grown up in Scotland. Always offering the lads tea.

The man was more stand-offish, and the wife too. We expected that though. I saw all the women leave that morning, off in the Range Rover. Going swimming. We were fencing and putting in paths, finishing off, four of us, down their land working away. Tidying up really. It was hot, a still day, not a breath of wind.

'It was after lunch and I went up towards the house to the toilet. I heard the dog barking, barking. I called out because it felt strange. Wrong. There was no one else there. Just this silence. I went over to the garage where the sound was coming from, but the main door was pulled down and locked. You could definitely hear the dog inside. Yap, yap. Then I remembered there was a side door through the house and so I went round to the kitchen and went inside calling out. No one answered – though his car was still there on the driveway. Inside the house the door to the garage was shut but not locked.

'So I went in. And then I saw him. Just inches off the ground. Four or five inches. He wasn't wearing any socks and the feet were awful. Purple looking. Your mind goes blank. The husband. The dog was barking at him but not touching. Keeping his distance, like the dog knew something was not right. The first thing in my head was, "I've got to get the dog to shut up." I couldn't think. I couldn't remember any numbers, the police, the ambulance. I just couldn't. It wasn't a rope either. It was an orange extension cord, flex. The cord was wrapped three times round a beam and the other end round his neck in a slip knot. His head had slipped to the side on his shoulder and there was dribble, mucus, from his mouth. One of the eyes was open and the lips were blue. He had wet himself. He was so close to ground you thought he was almost floating. The fella had hanged himself. Maybe the cable stretched out with his continued weight but it was like he almost could have reached the ground. Like on his tiptoes. I grabbed him but he was limp; he wasn't breathing. One of those computer chairs, with wheels, was just a few feet away – he must have stood on it and pushed himself off. I pushed that back under him to take weight but he just swung away. The dog kept barking so I ran back to the lads. One of them had a phone and we called 999. I went back in with the foreman. He checked for breath with his hand and we tried to see if there was a pulse. I thought we should cut him down but he said no as the man was dead. All the lads came up to have a look but the foreman ordered them out. We grabbed the dog and put him outside.

'After a time the police arrived. First one car then another. And the woman came back with the children. We were told to stay by the police because they wanted statements. Then one of policemen must have told her as I heard her scream. "Oh let me see him. I've got to see him, please, please let me see him." She started pleading with the sergeant. You could hear her almost shouting. But he wouldn't let her – and the ambulance arrived. She quietened down and nothing happened for ages. Then the ambulance reversed back inside the garage – they must have found the keys. Then it drove out a few yards and stopped. I could not really see – we were at the side to the right. They must have cut him down as then we heard her this time again roaring, screaming. "You useless fucker. Why, why, have you done this? What have you done to us? Useless man, useless man. You're a coward, a coward."

'The sergeant had let her into the ambulance. I could see it rock back and forth. She was slapping him, slapping the husband's body, the ambulance rocking back and forth. Hard. You could hear her fists, blows. The police and the ambulance crew just stood there, frozen. After five minutes the sergeant pulled her out. Her mother was in with her too. The ambulance drove away with the body and that was it.

'It was in the papers after. Months later. Something about loans gone wrong and people were after him. The thing I remember most was the look on the woman's face as she came out of the ambulance. The police, the crew, they were all afraid of her. No one would meet her eye. And no one said anything. But I saw her. A face like ice. Not a tear. Coldly angry. As angry as I have ever seen a woman with a man. Mad, mad at the dead man. She was like the Queen of Death.'

Jack stopped speaking. At first I thought it was just

a pause but then I realised this story was over. Jack sat back in the chair and his eyes flitted between his listeners looking for their reaction. For a long time, it seemed, no one in the huddle of watchers said anything until someone pulled out a cigarette packet and offered them round amongst the group. Noticing me, the smoker offered me one as well. I had stopped smoking years before but I took one, if only to be part of the group and earn my place. When I lit up, the nicotine went straight to my brain, the blood rushed in my ears and the drug-induced buzz made me light-headed. The conversation drifted away into another story about a court case and I lost the thread of it. I made an excuse and went off to the kitchen but really just to wander, stretch my legs, and clear my head.

In the kitchen were a couple of women, a mother and her younger married daughter and Nora, our close neighbour. The mother and daughter were from another village on the other side of the island, a few miles away. They introduced themselves – Ann and Sorcha. Ireland has become a land of short-haired women; fashion seems to dictate that as a woman ages her hair shortens. Ann's hair too was cut short above the shoulders and, with the extra weight of middle age, it was hard to tell how old she was, maybe mid-fifties. Sorcha had trailing brunette hair and looked more like a recent student. Nora was much older, a great grandmother, no taller than five foot, well into her eighties with a stern angular face. I wanted to make myself tea but all three women refused me any attempt to make it myself and gathered cups, milk and teabags, urging me to sit down as the kettle boiled. With the tea poured I joined them at the kitchen table. I had caught them mid-conversation but my presence passed as if unmarked.

'And how often were children buried there?' asked Sorcha.

'There is a *cillín* in every village. There's one in your own in Dugort too, close to the shore at the far end of the beach,' replied Nora.

I saw Sorcha look at her mother. 'At the end of the beach? We used to play there.'

'Everyone knew but no one talked of these things,' said Nora.

'*Cillín* were always set in sight of the water,' said Ann.

'They have always been there in those places,' said Nora.

'It's do with the spirits, though I can't explain why. I never liked them. Lonely spots.'

'And what does it mean, *cillín*?' said Sorcha

'In Irish it means "little burial ground",' said Nora.

'It's where they buried unbaptised babies. Or suicides. Or if they weren't sure. The church would not allow it. There is a *cillín* here in Dookinella, out there on a hill overlooking the strand, 200 yards from this house.'

'Here?' asked Sorcha.

'*Pasiti Marbh*,' said Nora.

There was a pause.

'How long . . .' Sorcha asked but Nora cut over her, ignoring the question.

'I buried Martin, my first born there. He was beautiful, blond curls.'

'You?' asked Sorcha, shocked.

'The priest ruled everything then. It was the 1950s. No one could speak out against them. He was born at six in the evening in the winter, December tenth. I was weak, the loss of blood. I held him in the bed beside me for a time. Michael, my husband, was away working in England. Maureen Barrett, our neighbour, got one of her lads to cycle to the Sound for the doctor, the old one. And he came out in his car. When he came to the house I remember his words in the room. He was harsh. "Take it away from her. It will only make her worse." "It", that is what he called my child. And so they did. I never saw him again, my baby boy. My grandfather buried Martin in the morning at first light in *Pasiti Marbh* in a Jacob's biscuit box. He had to do it.'

'The child . . .'

'He was stillborn. Perfect. I can still see his face, and the hair.'

There was a moment of stunned silence as the younger women stared at Nora.

'You couldn't have a burial in Slievemore?' asked Sorcha.

'Lazy bastards driving around in their cars. Priests. I've never forgiven them. Fat. Always asking for more money whilst our lads are away in England, killing themselves on the sites. Parasites, the whole fecking shower of them. You can take your priests and shove them up your arse.'

The shock of the fresh bitterness of the old woman's words stunned the table. Then Nora laughed out a low growl as if surprised at her own words: 'shove them up your arse'.

Ann burst out in laughter, seemingly licensed, at the earthy crudity and mockery of the pompous, frocked, dog-collared men who had for so long policed the parish and the land. Seeing her mother laugh, so did Sorcha, until all three women were guffawing. I joined in.

Pasiti Marbh is a flat, almost unmarked green slab of ground set on the foothills that rise toward Minaun at the end of the village. The *cillín*, overlooking the strand, is on common land – used as forage by the roving flocks of island sheep. There are no fences or boundaries, and unless you know what lies beneath your feet it would be easy to miss. Nor were there any names, distinguishable markers or lines of order, just a rough spread of flat stones covering over what must be individual baby graves. For those who know the nature of this place, *Pasití Marbh* always carries an air of ineradicable sadness. Each stone marks out loss and unrequited sorrow. No one knows how many children are buried here, dozens or more, or for how long such a burial site has been in use, maybe centuries; the memory of the unnamed fades with the passing generations.

Cillín are another wound in Irish history. Many of these burial grounds were originally pagan, but others were created to bury the banished dead; the unbaptised, suicides, heathens and heretics, anyone refused burial in consecrated ground by the Irish church. Most of the dead were stillborn babies born of carnal lust and hence stained by original sin. Theologically, these unbaptised infants were consigned neither to heaven nor hell but another realm – *Limbo Infantus*, darkness without pain. As a schoolboy, I remember being taught such doctrine from catechism books illustrated with cherubic, winged infants hovering within a realm of clouds.

The reality of the Catholic Church's prohibition on burial of the stillborn was far more cruel, a windswept scrap of land before the ocean, a pagan burial site on the margins and a crime of denial against the innocent dead. *Cillín* too were liminal spaces where the banished were seeded into the earth of their ancestral birth village, to be reclaimed and revisited by those who bore connection. To be remembered. I knew that one of my own aunts, a stillborn child of Sonny's mother, my paternal grandmother, Mary Barrett, was buried there though the child's exact gravesite was lost. That grandmother died before I was born and until Nora spoke I had never known anyone who had buried a child in *Pasití Marbh* herself. Such secret things, deemed almost shameful, were never spoken of aloud.

In the night of the wake, the boundaries by which we separate ourselves, the pasts we hoard, were breaking away and opening out. Sonny's corpse, his touchable deadness, had made it harder to deceive ourselves of the shiny lies of daylight. So for a few hours, at least, we were free of the constraints of our daily dissembling. Nora's story, like Jack's, was rising from the depths to the surface.

Something in me wanted to be on my own, listen to the sea and think about what I had heard. I stood up and walked to the other side of the room, looking out the glass sliding doors in the kitchen which faced the ocean. At the table the three women continued talking; Sorcha now asking questions of Nora, and her mother, Ann, seemingly nodding in agreement. They barely noticed I had left. Beyond the window the night remained still but was now clear. The tide was out and I could see the lights of the local town reflected on the wet strand across the curved bay, merging and mixing sea and land. One of the glass doors was open and the sound of distant surf mingled with the murmur of voices of the women and the watchers from the adjacent sitting room.

All my life I had stood apart and together, city and island, with these villagers. Divided. Unsure of who I was and to whom I belonged. Feeling I was a traitor beneath the skin. But now it no longer mattered. For in these late hours we had all reached back, becoming again who we always are, death's survivors, mortal soldiers, willingly exposing ourselves as vulnerable, anguished creatures. No longer strangers to each other in our mortality. In this company I would never be alone facing the terror I had felt in Bernard's death cubicle. Here the burden of death, others and our own, was shared out, talked over and tamed amongst the watchers and the wake-goers. We were already here calling out to each other, already sharing Sonny's death, and other deaths, together. In those close watching hours upon the corpse a portal had opened, too, amongst the living, and we spoke without fear on the nature of what each had seen and felt on the shores of life and death.

I went back in to see Sonny. The company in the sitting room were quieter now, resting. Blood sugars were low; the desire for sleep strong. There were maybe fifteen left in the quorum, gathered in bunches fending off sleep, a few softly talking amongst themselves. Others stared straight into the middle distance. It was close to three in the morning, the last stretch. Behind Sonny's head a taper burned, casting a flickering shadow on his face. I brushed my fingers through the shock of white hair that sprang back against my hand. And I touched his cheek, colder now than any human warm. He stayed dead.

Soon, whether you believed in the afterlife to come or not, Sonny would be leaving us. This was our last sharings as father and son, as brother, friend or neighbour. Nora wasn't wrong when she said Sonny was a fine-looking corpse. The agony of the cancer that had ravaged him in his final days had passed, and some of the father I knew had come back. But more than that I began to understand what Sonny always knew; his death and wake was not an ending but a further binding between the dead, the living and the dead-to-be. A gift. The watchers in the bedroom who had kept vigil, Hector's quorum who gathered here for Sonny's wake, were by their presence already girding themselves for their own deaths. The wake, amongst the oldest rites of humanity, was the best of the armour we would ever have. Today it was Sonny but it would soon be someone else, perhaps one of the old farmers who sat mute in the room. But it could be any of one of us if the Celestial Sniper took a shot. Standing beside my dead father, I felt stronger, already looking out at the far horizon, unafraid. Better to know life's end than live in fear and be engulfed without warning. As Sonny had shared time with many, many of the dead at wakes on the island, now he too shared his death for those who came after. What was there to fear? To breathe is to die. Death was alive in all of us but was no stranger here. It was Sonny's last lesson not just to his children but to all who came to his wake, a reminder; this is how we die.

I sat down on one of the bar stools. And it was then, partly obscured by another mourner, I first noticed him, out of the corner of my eye; a familiar stranger. He must have come through the front door when I was in the kitchen. The face I knew, his name tripping on my tongue. We had known each other as teenagers through whole summers of dances on the island. Back then he was, crucially, a bit older and owner of a precious car; a Ford Cortina that we would all pile into, girls and boys squashed on each other's laps, seven or eight of us in the back seat, for the journey back from the dance. With no taxis or public transport on the island, and no other means to get home from the dance halls seven miles away, he had been a good man to know. In Sonny's wake house, decades later, the same face had filled out, the hair was a bit thinner, and the sideburns gone. I knew him even though I hadn't seen him in more than twenty years. He reached out to shake my hand.

'Sorry for your trouble, Kevin. Do you remember me?' and then he smiled.

'I do,' I said, stumbling.

'How did you get on with that girleen in the end? Sinead?' he asked.

There was a teasing smile on his face and then I couldn't stop laughing, either.

'And do you remember the last wake we were at together?'

'How could I forget? Eamon,' his name coming back to me in a flash.

And we both laughed.

I was fifteen and spent most of that summer jammed between bodies in an island dance hall, the Wavecrest Ballroom, madly in pursuit of girls and romance. In daylight the Wavecrest was a scruffy oblong barn-like building marooned in a dismal car park on the western end of the island. The last dance hall before America. But in the sultry dark on a hot August night the Wavecrest was a cornucopia of desire, a palace of coloured lights, rotating disco balls, the clash of a hundred cheap perfumes and the mingling of a thousand bodies. Entertainment was powered by a cavalcade of live bands belting out cover versions of every hit from Elvis, the Beatles, Tom Jones, to last week's *Top of the Pops*, at awesome volume until two in the morning. Drink, boldness, lust, teenage ineptitude and rampant desire all played their part. The dance floor filled with gyrating couples and sexual longing. The sheer throng of swinging limbs and energy expended raised temperatures to sauna-like levels. Sweat soaked through high-collared shirts, denim jackets, miniskirts and maxi dresses and ran off bodies in torrents to the waxed floor.

There were some old-fashioned rules. Each dance was a 'set', three songs in a row, that allowed a few seconds of audible conversation in between numbers to charm the object of your desire. If you failed, as I most often did, your would-be girlfriend was free to walk off disinterested and return to her friends. But if there was a spark of interest you would dance on into the next set, hoping the lead singer would soon programme a 'slow set' and you could clinch up, sweaty body to body. More serious teenage entanglements could then be pursued in the 'mineral bar' downstairs, which sold soft drinks. Beyond the mineral bar was the welcoming darkness of the car park for a furtive snog and a tentative fumble.

On that particular night, myself and my would-be date Sinead – fifteen, blonde, heavy mascara, wearing a yellow chiffon dress – had signalled a mutual interest by holding ourselves a little too tightly, thigh to thigh, on the floor as the last dance was called and the Irish national anthem played. It was too late. Within moments the main lights, a blaze of fluorescence, came on and the ballroom's side doors opened like a freezer drawer to vent the sweat-bound heat and chill ardent desire. The night was over and another hunt for a lift to avoid a seven-mile walk home began in earnest.

My getting-a-lift-home technique was rudimentary; abandon any male companions and hang close to the girls – who obviously were far more likely to get a lift from distant cousins or the driver boyfriends of their elder sisters. So I chatted away with Sinead and her friends. And then Eamon came over to join us. I knew Eamon, but at the time didn't realise he had gravitated to the sexual superstar status of being the owner of a car.

'Shall we go back to the wake for the craic?' he asked.

It was some opening line. Going to a wake for the craic, rollicking with a corpse in the room, was unknown territory for me. The decision was made by Sinead.

'Why don't we?' she answered boldly, looking directly at me.

I had no idea what was going on. But as a proposition, going on to the wake was irresistible. I'd get a lift towards home. The night would go on and I would still be with Sinead. And I was hungry. And there was nowhere else to go as by now, nearly three in the morning, the whole island was shut up. We piled into Eamon's Ford Cortina, Sinead on my lap in back, crowded next to Mairead, Maureen, Patrick, Mick and Sheila, until the vehicle could hold no more.

Once we were clear of the dance crowd, the road was empty and the strip of island villages thralled in sleep. It was a clear moonlit night, almost full. The sharp shadows of houses by the side of the road ran black or deep blue in the casting light. The ocean, below us on the right-hand side of the road, glimmered silver. The road unfolded like a strip of silence that drew us forward and closed behind us as if we were the last on earth to be left alive. For a while no one spoke; we listened instead to the growl of the engine. Squashed against one of the back passenger doors, but with the sensuous weight of Sinead on my lap, the heat of her body on mine, I would have driven on and on until the road ran out. Then Eamon broke in with a joke to one of the boys. The moment passed and we were all joshing teenagers again, teasing over who had danced with who.

We arrived at one of the flat-roofed houses dating from the 1950s. It was a square box with a central door and, like lighted eyes, windows on either side. The lights on in both these front rooms, and the other cars parked outside, marked it out as a wake house. We opened the garden gate, walking up the narrow concrete path in file and into the house. Unsure of what to do, I followed along, copying everyone else's actions.

Inside, the house was unadorned painted walls, lino on the floor, a turf and ashes bucket by the door, a pair of turned-down women's wellingtons close by to avoid bringing dirt into the house from the field and the turf heap. We turned sharp right into what must have been a sitting room but now held the coffin and other mourners. The air was thick with cigarette smoke. With Eamon at the lead we shuffled our way towards the corpse. We shook hands solemnly with the dead man's middle-aged daughters, Rose and Breda, garbling our 'Sorry for your trouble's before an obligatory blessing of ourselves at the head of the coffin. All the holy statues in the house, a nine-inch baby Jesus dressed up as a little prince as the Child of Prague, an eighteen-inch tall china Saint Bernadette in her brown nun's habit and a smaller glazed Virgin Mary, in blue and white, had been gathered in a cupboard next to the coffin to create a make-shift altar. In front of the statues three candles burned in small red glass jars.

Seamus wasn't looking great. In his final illness his liver must have packed up and the skin had the yellowish look of the heavily jaundiced. Incongruously, he was dressed in a beige suit with newly bought dark blue carpet slippers – to be soft on his feet, we were later told, in his new projected heavenly realm; there having been no matching brown slippers in stock on the day. Close up, looking down on Seamus in the coffin, the most striking thing was his nostril hair which hung comically in two walrus-like tusks from his sallow bloodless nostrils. Seamus's layer-outer had also forgotten to trim the rest of the old man's facial hair, which also sprouted from his ears in a wiry mini-forest.

There was a leaden atmosphere in the room. The chorus of wailing women had long departed or lapsed into dry-eyed exhaustion. Seamus's corpse had either been hanging around for too long or his daughters were now too exhausted to shed further tears on his behalf. We soon gathered that, even in his daughters' eyes, Seamus was being classified as a 'happy corpse' as in:

'Sure, isn't it happy for him . . .' leaving unspoken the final words of relief: '. . . and for us that he is dead.'

Seamus had been a misery; his wife was long gone and he had suffered a withering stroke a decade before. With a gammy leg but grimly hanging on, he had drained away the well of filial love, stumbling ever so slowly but ever more needily towards his maker. Looking down at him in his coffin, I remembered seeing a lone brooding figure on a seat outside in the front garden, idling the hours watching traffic zip by, but never engaging with passersby on the road. Perhaps the stroke had affected Seamus's speech, shutting him off, dwindling into himself day after day. The shuffling off of his mortal coil was a quiet blessing and his wake a formal ceremonial.

After our pretend prayers, we sat down in a group, just feet from the yellowed corpse, an influx of slightly tipsy, giggling teenagers. We were soon offered tea and ham sandwiches. As we were waiting on the tea to brew, Breda came round with an open plate of cigarettes. I watched in amazement as Patrick, one of the other boys in the car, brazenly swiped two extra cigarettes as the plate was passed along the narrow rows. Emboldened by Patrick, one of the girls, Sheila, filched another couple for herself. Rose then appeared with a small plate of snuff and left it with us to pass round. Snuff was common in the wakes of my childhood but I had never tried it. Dared by Eamon to have a go, I pinched a wedge of the dark brown dust between my fingers and snorted it up my nose. The acid burn in my right nostril provoked an explosive coughing fit and guffaws of stifled laughter from my friends. When the sandwiches came round we all tucked in with the famishment of teenagers, scoffing plate after plate of ham sandwiches until more were brought out. Eamon even asked, straight-faced, for a refill of tea, saying his throat was almost as parched as 'Seamus's there'.

Squirming at Eamon's blatant mockery of the corpse, we practically pissed ourselves trying not to burst out in open laughter. Weirdly, Eamon's testing demands were met with a bland, unseeing acquiescence by Rose and Breda. An extra cup of tea for Eamon soon arrived.

The real craic though was just about to begin. From his pocket Eamon pulled a small button, like the button on a man's suit, and held it in his hand.

'Let's play the Ring.'

No one bothered to explain the rules but it was obvious everyone had played the game before. Eamon put the button between his vertically flattened palms and went down the line from boy to girl, hovering over each player who held their palms in a similar position. There were nine of us from the car, five girls and four boys, and Eamon dropped the button from his palm in secret into the pressed together hands of one of the other players. The Ring was a simple guessing game as to who now held the button, but with a painful forfeit for the wrong answer. As leader, Eamon asked each player in turn and doled out punishments. If you were male, the penalty was a rap on the back of your knuckles. You had to hold your clenched fist aloft and Eamon, who could have worked as a circus strongman judging by his strength, struck down hard with two extended knuckles onto the back of your hand. It felt like being hit by a metal rod, the soft skin easily bruising. The penalty for girls was a sexual forfeit. A losing female player had to go outside for five minutes with a boy chosen by Eamon. The questions, blows and staged disappearances out the back door, went on until the holder of the button was discovered and a new round of the game begun.

The Ring was a wake game, an echo of the funeral games played by the ancient Greeks in the *Iliad*, and one of hundreds documented in Ireland over the last four centuries. Wake games were either punishing competitive trials of strength between male contestants or sacrilegious derision of Catholic sacraments like confession. Mock marriages and kissing games incited libidinous foreplay that often ended in sexual intercourse. Led by a male *cleasái* player and master of misrule, wake games are a defiant usurpation of our mortality and a licensing of orgiastic excess. In opposition to the *mná caointe*, with their promise of engulfing feminine renewal, the male *cleasaidhe* was a jester-like figure who mocked the dead and the prevailing social order. By acting out, playing games around the corpse, the *cleasái* helped unleash some of our own deepest longings. The coldness of a corpse has its own perverse existential aphrodisiac; nothing so encourages the animal within us, the hunger for sexual consummation, the need of the comfort of another warm body, than death's present denial. We affirm ourselves in heat and flesh.

Wake games are an old message passed down; our lives flow in a mortal tide; cast aside disapproving priests and parents, seize this moment of selfish, sensual pleasure for yourself. Wakes on the island were often rated by the young for their *prumsaí* – courting games and fun. Our version of Ring was tame compared to the wake games of the seventeenth century.

And now came tobacco and pipes, and sneezing . . .
The room large as it was soon filled with clouds of
smoke, which made the small candles give so faint
a light as if they were just going out. The elder sort
sat belching or sneezing, while a lusty young fellow

snatches a woman's shawl from her head, and ties it about his hat as a distinguishing mark of his office among them. Then as captain or master of misrule he selected a band of about a dozen young fellows who hauled out so many women of the younger sort for their mates; and by these were the rudest, most unpolished and barbarous sorts of sports used that ever were seen, especially in such a place where such an object of mortality lay; to which not one that I saw showed the least regard. Sometimes they followed one another in a ring (as they say the fairies do) in a rude dance to the music of the bagpipe, and as a great jest sometimes they made excursions upon some old body who maybe was nodding and it passed very well. After this they betook themselves to another sort of play, where one fellow ran his head between the thighs of another and so hoist him on his shoulders whilst a third clapped his buttocks till they were (surely) sore. If any stranger were to make a judgement of the other customs of the Irish by this one of waking their dead, he might justly reckon them among the rudest and most beastly people in the world.

John Dunton, the seventeenth-century English bookseller, never saw those Irish revellers were celebrating life, not decrying the dead, at the wake. Centuries later we played out the same life song. We sniggered at wrong answers and half muffled our cries of pain as Eamon's hand came down on another loser. We burst out in suppressed laughter at a girl or boy's embarrassment. We flirted. We teased and mocked and smoked far too many of the free cigarettes being doled out and figured how to pair up with the partner of our desire. Seamus, being dead, made no objection to the noise or our revelry. But neither did his daughters, Rose and Breda. Or any of the elderly mourners, the old men hunkered down, who sat in the quorum around us. Not even a hostile glance. As if this ritual of *prumsaí*, life's renewal, was part of Seamus's departing.

Playing Ring whilst waking the dead has a price. The back of my hand ached for days afterwards, bruised black from a string of wrong answers. But it was worth it. Because out in the moonlit dark at the back of Seamus Gallagher's wake house, paying forfeit, I first laid my lips on Sinead's tremulous mouth. The dead man in the box had only heightened rather than deterred our hormonal urges.

Eamon's teasing was a jolt back to my teenage summers on the island and the mingling of life and death together. Bernard's death had sent me on the wrong odyssey, hunting in the wilderness, for something that was always within my grasp here at home on the island. I settled in to catch up on the path of Eamon's life and explain my own. And ask about Sinead's.

'Of course I remember Seamus's wake. Where is Sinead now?'

'Oh, she's married to an English fella, living in England, near Preston. She has two children. I saw her home a year or two ago.'

Time passed, but it was not long before the first beams of the morning sun broke over the foothills of Minaun, striking the stones of Sonny's own fireplace. Across the bay the rosy-fingered dawn was lighting up the eastward face of Croaghaun mountain, drenching the heather in a warm red glaze. The sun was rising again in the east and a new day had begun And Sonny's soul had, Heaven or Hades or not, taken flight.

From the kitchen came a bustle of plates and the smell of frying bacon. Hector's quorum, or the 'stickers' as they are known, are rewarded for their labours guarding the Gates of Chaos by a full Irish fried breakfast. In shifts we were soon sitting down to thick rashers of bacon, sausages, toast and jam, and mugs of scalding hot tea. And then alone or in small groups, my mortal brothers left their stations, my father's wake, walking out into the soft light of the ocean shore and another day of life.

Hector was waked for nine days, but Sonny's wake, like most islanders, lasted for two days sandwiched around one all-night vigil. Some families, waiting on relatives coming from America or England, will run a wake for longer. After catching a few hours' sleep, I came back in the early afternoon for more mourning. The chorus of women had reassembled, the flow of visitors continuing, but the mood had flattened. The keening was more restrained, the tears fewer. We were settling into Sonny's deadness. More teas were offered and drank, cigarettes smoked, sandwiches eaten. Towards five in the evening the numbers began to swell for the removal of the remains; another bridge of parting.

The sitting room filled with forty people and the priest returned to say the rosary. The crowd dispersed outside to wait in the front garden. Inside we were left as family members to say our final goodbyes; to kiss Sonny for the last time and brush his hair. I noticed Teresa, in tears, slip some personal mementoes, a child's toy – grave gifts – into the coffin. It was time to close the lid. I helped Ted place the top on the coffin and together we hand-turned the four crucifix screws down on Sonny. And then with my brothers and sisters we lifted Sonny onto our shoulders and walked out through the front door into the garden. Two chairs had been placed on the green grass of the lawn and we laid him down perched between them. It was a soft evening, warm sunshine, good weather for a final goodbye.

After a lifetime of coming and goings from this island, our island of perpetual exile, Sonny was leaving Dookinella, in body and spirit, to go forever to his final resting place. We stood together, sons, daughters, sisters, neighbours, mourners and mortals, amidst the fuchsia and the pampas grass, and sang out in unison a last prayer, an antiphon from the old Latin liturgy, *In paradisum.*

> May the angels lead you into paradise: may the martyrs receive you at your arrival and lead you into the holy city of Jerusalem. May the choirs of angels receive you and with Lazarus, once a poor man, may you find eternal rest.

The dog-collared priest, who led the prayers, unflinchingly joined too in the far older pagan rite of splashing the coffin and the walls of the house with Holy Water to bar Sonny's soul, troubled or not, from ever returning to our family hearth.

After the priest finished, we lifted Sonny's coffin up again on our shoulders and one of my aunts, invoking another unknown pagan spirit ritual, kicked over the chairs just to make sure the bridge of return was doubly broken. We loaded Sonny into the hearse and drove slowly towards the church at the crossroads, a mile away.

With the hearse parked, we loaded Sonny up again on our shoulders. The church was filled with islanders even for this short ceremonial. We, his daughters and sons, took the weight, bore the burden, of our father's coffin, slowly swaying forward down the aisle to the spot where his body would rest for the night near the altar, slipping away into the embrace of the Catholic Church.

Sonny would have been pleased, a final tribal reckoning: an ordinary man who had done more good than harm; a builder who had left something behind; a father who had reopened the road; an exile who had come Home. This small journey, moving forward 200 paces, step by step, down the aisle, together and apart, in this the last act of his fatherhood, was also a new mark within our own lives. Almost all of his children were now fathers and mothers. Sonny's weight on our collarbones led us on far beyond the altar, unshielded from death's horizon, towards our own mortal shore.

The following morning we came for Mass, the priest using incense and a swinging censer to mask the high sweet scent of death and decay rising from Sonny's coffin. And then we bore Sonny again out of the church, into the hearse, and, in a long cavalcade of cars, took the road up through the gorse hedgerows towards the old graveyard on the foothills of Slievemore. Sonny's last journey. Nearly 300 villagers, family and clan, came with us to the grave, the line of parked cars stretching back along the narrow road towards the ocean. If you looked to the east, their stones glimmering in the sunlight, you could see the ruins of the old village of Dookinella, nestled below Minaun, where he had been born.

On the mountain, the path to the grave was steep, tight and narrow, encumbered by other tombs. But with the steadying hand of the chief gravedigger, Sonny's old friend Mikey Dan, behind us, and a close cousin Pat Jack at our side, we carried the coffin through the maze of headstones and up the hillside.

On the island there are no professional gravediggers, just local village men who volunteer; a self-perpetuating squad of four or six who insist on digging the grave by hand with shovels and whose only reward is a few drinks afterwards at The Crossroads Inn. Digging six feet down in the rocky ground is a tough job, a day's labour, but all those asked regard this burden as an honour. A debt to the dead that will in time be repaid in many ways. An act of grace. At the grave I was again struck how these seemingly humble men moved with a deft purpose, so sure of their element; clearing pathways through the crowd for the moving coffin; presiding over the final leaving as the coffin was lowered; and all eagerly willing to bear their share of the task.

In the tight confines of the crowded graveyard, we put Sonny's coffin down over the gouge in the earth that was his grave; the weight of the coffin resting on three strong timber sleepers to prevent it falling in. We said a few more Catholic prayers, a final verse of the rosary in Irish, but we were here to finish this work, this burial. When it was time, Mikey Dan told us to pick up the three long ropes that had been stretched across the grave under the coffin. Each of the six pallbearers, on either side of the grave, lifted the ropes snug under the coffin, grasping their rough tread in our hands. Once we sure we were ready we nodded, and then Mikey gave the final command, the very last physical burden of the living towards the dead.

'Take the weight.'

We heaved on the ropes bearing Sonny's coffin as the gravediggers pulled the wooden supports away. And then slowly, ever so slowly, directed by Mikey and in unison, we lowered the coffin down, letting the ropes burn through our hands, down and down, until the coffin rested deep on the brown earth.

Some families leave the filling of the grave to the gravediggers, but we had decided to take a turn, the men in the family dressed in suits and ties, shovelling the earth from the nearby mound back into the grave, shovel after shovel, until it was done. And the grave filled and Sonny's dying over. Finished.

At the graveside more people came to us and offered their condolences.

'Sorry for your trouble.'

And shook my hand. I was grateful now for these repeated small offerings, their time and the petrol consumed. What else can be expected? The mourners had given up a few hours of their own lives to share in this sorrow, to stand with us, the bereaved, in an hour of need, and affirm that we were not alone in death. What more can one ask for? And if such unselfish acts of compassion are not a form of love, of hope, an open, selfless recognition of our universal nature, then what is?

HOW TO LOVE, LIVE AND DIE

You cannot step twice into the same river, ever newer waters flow around and beneath your feet. And we cannot all go back to the island, listen daily to the cowboy songs and the 'deaths' on the radio, and live on and die in the last full gatherings of this ancient Celtic rite. But we can carry much of the Irish Wake with us in our hearts. A rite that survived the fall of Troy and a thousand generations before the rise of the Western Death Machine can easily survive the retransplantation back to our cities of glass and concrete. We need to find our way again with death.

For a million years, our forebears managed to die all by themselves without hospitals, mortuaries, undertakers, prepaid funeral plans and the Western Death Machine. The Neolithic people who buried their dead on the high slopes of Slievemore 6,000 years ago probably coped with death better than we do. Why would our ancestors, who had only stones for tools, haul huge slabs of rock and build communal tombs that were used for centuries, unless they believed the bodies of their dead were important? Why would they have laboured if they did not love their dead? And why did they go on living so close to the graves of their ancestors unless they believed in a bond between the dead and the living?

To be human is to be mortal, and to be mortal is to love, live and die amidst the lives of everyone around you on the island or in the city. And to embrace rather than deny our mortal fate. Sonny wanted to live not die, but when he discovered he had no choice he knew how to die. And Sonny knew this, too: if you never know sorrow then you will never know love and if you never know death then you never know life.

On the island, death still calls in an ancient voice, louder and wiser, than our Whisper Death World. The island may be far away, but that voice is close if you want to listen. Everything you need is within your grasp to rediscover the oldest lessons of humanity; how to love someone other than yourself, how to live through their death and how to face your own death with the aid of your community. Waking with the dead is a good place to start learning those lessons again.

If you can find yourself a decent Irish Wake to go to, just turn up and copy what everyone else is doing. Don't be nervous. Being there and taking part is the main thing. And don't be shy. Go up to the bereaved, shake their hand and tell them: 'Sorry for your trouble.'

You will be surprised how glad they are to see you. Death, remember, is our great leveller. We are all equal, all mortal, all brothers and sisters. There are no strangers, only fellow travellers.

Be sure to touch the flesh of the corpse for that ever-wondrous ice-cube-in-a-rubber-glove feeling of a dead human. And use the touch to rediscover for yourself how we, the living, are everything and nothing like our dead kin.

Relax, have a cup of tea, a chat with other mourners, have a drink, a bit of food, and start getting yourself accustomed to the very ordinariness of it all. One day, for sure, you will be in the same sort of box. Dead on Arrival, somewhere.

Take your kids along too if you can. Learning how to die is just a foreign language – the younger you start the easier it gets. Children are usually especially beloved at funerals, for they are our future.

If you can't find a wake begin with a little practice on your own:

Make a phone call to a dying uncle and ask how he is.

Go visit the sick, the terminally ill, and be prepared to talk about anything; their worries, their football team, their treatment, their hopes, the weather, what they think is going to happen to the plants in the front garden, their denial, the funeral arrangements, the World Series, whatever. Don't be too surprised if they either just talk endlessly about their illness or don't mention it at all and talk about movies instead. Don't wait. Go visit. Have that conversation now as you won't talk about anything when they are dead.

Don't go because you think you are being 'charitable' or 'kind' and will get some sort of brownie points in heaven. Go selfishly for yourself as well, to get a glimpse of what it's like – dying – and to get a feel for the landscape. Offer yourself to help with another's dying. Practice will improve your own performance.

If you are the one doing the dying, don't be afraid to share your death. Reach out and invite your relatives and old friends to see you to say goodbye. If you can face your own death, tell everyone you are dying. Ask for their help. Most of them will feel honoured to be asked. If you can't – don't be too hard on yourself. You are allowed to choose. Denial or not, dying is exhausting, so get help where you can.

Find yourself a *bean chabrach*, a midwife of death, a son, a daughter, a husband, a wife, a friend, who will be with you in your dying and take responsibility when you are no longer able. The world will go on without you, so order your affairs, wills, properties, unresolved conflicts, as best as you are able to protect those you still love. Forgive yourself, too, if you can't.

If you can accept the mystery of yourself, the who

you were and are still, and not the dream you thought you wanted to be, then do so.

If you are a relative or friend and care enough, be there for the dying days. There is nothing else in your life that will probably ever be as important. More real. Be there for the hour of death and remember to pray for your own in the moment.

The dead belong to those who loved them. So go see the dead, particularly your own dead, for Priam's heart-comforting. Refuse to be fobbed off by officials and the Western Death Machine, whatever they say about procedures and the body of your beloved. The Trojans never embalmed Hector and who are these strangers to know what is your heart's comforting? Remember – if shared DNA, love and grief don't count with the bodies of the dead, then neither does their petty authority.

Touch the flesh of the dead. Brush their hair. Kiss them if you wish. Hold them in your arms. Spend some time in their company. Look like you are praying over the corpse – you won't be doing any harm whatever your religion, even if you are an atheist. If you can, pray for the peaceful repose of their soul. And pray selfishly, too, for yourself.

Hug the bereaved. Stay with them night and day. Bring some shopping and help shift the furniture. Have a wake. Hang around and help with the tea and sandwich making. Join in the *mná caointe*. Do some keening and some crying. Look at the corpse. Volunteer to join Hector's quorum and man the Gates of Chaos to guard the passage out of this departing soul. Funerals can be sad but they are often great craic too. Enjoy the *prumsaí*. Relax. Have a feast and some drink. Share some stories of life and death.

Go to more funerals and take your children with you. Offer to bear the honour of carrying the dead to the grave.

When you go home from the cold of the grave, hold your children in your arms and enjoy the wonder of being alive. Talk to your children about death, the dead, and life.

Make love to another warm human body to satiate the animal hunger inside you – the existential fear we all rightly have of the cold grave. You will never feel more alive.

Go out of your way to cross the office floor and shake the hand of the bereaved and offer your condolences. They won't be surprised or upset because they already are grieving. Offer whatever help you can.

Speak of the dead who shaped your life more often,

so that your children know of them and that their remembrance lives on in you, just as you hope your own
remembrance will live on in the lives of others. Visit
their graves.

And lastly, remember – take the weight.

As the coarse rope under Sonny slipped and burned
through my palms, and I strained on Slievemore mountain with the weight of my father's body in his coffin,
I knew what I had missed in failing to bind the wound
of Bernard's death and in all my death-wandering in
other worlds. The only way to take the weight of my
own mortality was through offering to take the weight
of others. I could face death by reaching into the ordinary lives, dyings and deaths of the others around me.
And together help them bear their burden, in the same
way that we lowered Sonny's coffin in unison, lighten-
ing the weight. I could share my death, as Sonny had,
within a community, because others before me had the
grace to share theirs. Death was nothing strange or
terrifying, but a constancy within life. Another act of
mundane fearlessness.

You might be asking yourself now:
Is that it?
*A few pious words, trite formulas, after a few hundred
pages?*

But words are not the test here. It is our actions that define our understanding, our fear, of death. Ask yourself again:

When did you last see, touch, a real dead body?
Go to a funeral?
Sit with the bereaved and ask them how it feels?
Talk with the dying?
Or talk about dying?

Do your answers fit in a world where everyone dies?

Back the shore at Dookinella, on the strand, the ocean waters are cold, the rip current is strong, and it takes time, courage and practice to dive into the oncoming green Atlantic breakers and learn to embrace the elements. Free yourself from the fear. It's harder than you think to break away from the blinding of the Western Death Machine. In fact, it's the work of a lifetime.

Most of us will, in time, live out an ordinary life like Sonny did and will never be called upon to be a hero. Our Sun will rise early in the east and one day fall, forever, in the west, in a world unmoved by our individual fate. Our lives, however we define them, will be our own, quiet responsibility. And so too will be the moment when death comes for the first or a further time; a neighbour, a friend, a lover, a child. We will all be asked in those moments to take the weight. To be truly human is to bear the burden of our own mortality and to strive, in grace, to help others carry theirs; sometimes lightly and sometimes courageously. In communally accepting death into our lives we will all relearn the first and oldest lessons of humankind. How to be brave in irreversible sorrow. How to love someone other than ourselves. How to reach out and share this mortal life with the dying, the dead and the bereaved. How to go on living no matter how great the rupture or unexpected the loss of those loved. How to face our own death. And how to teach your children to face their deaths.

A wake, the public display of a corpse and the support of your community, remains the best inoculation yet invented against the terrors of anomie, the great maw of alienating fear that strikes those close to unexpected death when the whole world crumbles into meaninglessness. If you've never touched a dead body then the first sight of a corpse, your sister or your father, will be a mortal terror. But if you have been seeing, touching the dead since you were a child, like the cherubic little girls who played at the feet of Sonny's coffin, you will recognise something older; the very ordinary dead. You will know the world does not fall apart for the death of kings and presidents, fathers or mothers or your beloved child. Or you.

Perhaps the Irish Wake is not enough. No amount of 'Sorry for your trouble' will ever bring back the warm limbs of a familiar lover, return Hector from the grave, resurrect your mother or stave off grief for a lost child. But like the islanders who kept vigil day and night with Sonny as he sank towards death, and then kept vigil again over his dead body, it is all we can possibly offer. We offer ourselves, our living presence, our mortal kinship, or we offer nothing at all.

We could of course go on doing nothing. Shun the sick and dying, never talk of death or see or touch their bodies. Shut our ears to the sound of keening women, cross the road to avoid the bereaved, and carry around a lie in our hearts that we have no need of the comfort of other mortals because death will somehow never happen. But, believe me, it will.

A couple of centuries after the poet Homer died, another Greek philosopher, Heraclitus, wrote: 'It is men who are immortal not the Gods; dying in each other's life and living in each other's death.'

And he was right. Zeus and all the other gods of Homer's *Iliad* have faded in time. But we mortals remain, struggling within ourselves, generation to generation, to answer the same questions; how to live, how to love and how to die. The wound we bear in grief is the same wound we bear in being human.

Whenever I come home to the island, I always visit the ruins of the old village of Dookinella, the tumble-down drystone walls, the nettle-sprouted interiors, the maze of small lanes that ran with human and animal traffic. Almost everything is gone, the roofs, the doors, the windows. Every scrap of wood, every fencepost or metal peg, every once-was, has rotted away or turned relic, like a bone picked clean, a skeleton. This village, perched on the edge of the world before the great ocean, was never seen as an important place, and the ordinary lives of all those who were born, lived, went into exile or died here passed unnoticed by a wider world. A forgotten tomb.

But this fallen village, and the other living villages that have replaced it on the island, are very important places. For thousands of years these villages were and are the last living archives of the oldest faith of humanity. The very same faith that Homer wrote about, too, in the *Iliad*, when he spoke of glorious battles and the clash of heroes on the plains of Troy. And the keening of the bereaved and the heart-comforting of a dead son in his father's arms. And a dead father in his son's arms. A faith that tells us, no matter how great the loss, how shattering the death, that we can stand together with the bereaved, wake our dead, lay them to rest and heal up our mortal wound.

It has been the greatest of my life's honours to take my place in Hector's perpetual quorum at my father's wake, and man the portals again of the natural world to guard the safe passage out of a departing ordinary soul. To join with my fellow mortal soldiers, brothers and sisters, in victory or defeat, grief and sorrow, sadness or secret joy, and brace ourselves together on the shore against the mortal wave of death's ocean.

To take the weight and openly affirm again what is and ever will be the very last, best hope of all humanity, that we shall not love, live or die alone.

May you too find in death the same grace I found in my father's wake.

ACKNOWLEDGEMENTS

On a remote Irish island, close to shore, at the bedside of a dying man, in the company of the *mná caointe*, with the sound of the rosary booming off the ceiling, I felt both the revelation and the burden of *My Father's Wake* descend on my shoulders. I saw a way of dealing with death that dwelt amongst us as far back as the fall of Troy, long before the blinding of our Western Death Machine. My task was to help with the remembering.

In my all death hunting, I have been often graced by the kindness, generosity and painful heart-exposed honesty of hundreds of other lives. I hope the words here offered will be a reward for the time vested in a passing stranger and my debt in some measure repaid. Now my work is done. My promise, to the best of my ability, fulfilled and the work of others begun – to judge these words and journeys amongst the living and the dead and act upon them if they so wish.

All that is described within these pages is true, and has been lived or lost. To protect the living and dead, names and places have been changed, and the chronologies of time altered, and I have no apology for this.

The river of understanding flows beneath and above the earth and returns, often, back on itself.

I know the recounting will not necessarily be easy or comfortable for every reader. I wish this was not so but the wisdom I have learnt from my fathers and mothers on the island directly challenges, sometimes painfully, the denial that surrounds death in the Western world.

May you live your life in the light and not be touched by the worst of these seen and felt sorrows. And may you too find in death the grace I discovered so present in the Irish Wake.

I remain eternally grateful for and to the continuing keepers of an ancient faith and my many mothers and fathers on the island, living or dead, including Michael Cafferkey, Thomas Gielty, Kathleen Gielty, Bridget Gielty, Michael Dan Gallagher, Edward and Nellie Toolis, my maternal grandparents Matilda and Pat Martin Gallagher, my grandfather Patrick Toolis and my birth mother Mary Gallagher. I am, too, obligated to my sisters Teresa, Ria and Angela Toolis, my brother Francis, my sister-in-law Marie and my aunts Mary, Margaret and Kathleen Toolis and Tilda McGuinness. On the journey, I have lost both brother and sister mortal soldiers Martin O'Hagan, Lawrence Gardner, Katy Jones, Bernard and Martin. Many friends have aided in the creation, rumination and reading of the manuscript, including but not limited to Siobhán Garrigan, Justin Basquille, Hugh Jordan, Jenny Matthews,

John McHugh, Morag Prunty and Tommy Johnston. I owe a debt for my own life on a number of occasions to my friend Abu Mahdi, and for the late-night journeys at speed through the Jordan Valley to Jerusalem. Long ago and far away, Jimmy 'Fingers' also helped a frightened child endure the living tomb of Male Chest. I would like to thank my agent, Sam Copeland, and editors Jenny Lord, Holly Harley and Bea Hemming in helping the book into existence.

I remain indebted too to the Irish Arts Council, when many doors were closed, for financially supporting the time of the writing; true courage is not the endorsement of success but the precarious investment in the spirited unknown. The risk.

I hope I have proved worthy of that act of faith.

Kevin Toolis,
Dookinella, 2017